EMERGING
MARKETS
RULE

GROWTH STRATEGIES OF
THE NEW GLOBAL GIANTS

EMERGING
MARKETS
RULE

MAURO F. GUILLÉN
and
ESTEBAN GARCÍA-CANAL

New York Chicago San Francisco Lisbon London Madrid Mexico City
Milan New Delhi San Juan Seoul Singapore Sydney Toronto

1 2 3 4 5 6 7 8 9 0   DOC/DOC   1 8 7 6 5 4 3 2

ISBN: 978-0-07-179811-2
MHID: 0-07-179811-0

e-ISBN: 978-0-07-179812-9
e-MHID: 0-07-179812-9

This publication is designed to provide accurate and authoritative information in regard to the subject matter covered. It is sold with the understanding that neither the author nor the publisher is engaged in rendering legal, accounting, or other professional service. If legal advice or other expert assistance is required, the services of a competent professional person should be sought.
> —*From a Declaration of Principles Jointly Adopted by a Committee of the American Bar Association and a Committee of Publishers and Associations*

Library of Congress Cataloging-in-Publication Data

Guillén, Mauro F.
    Emerging markets rule : growth strategies of the new global giants / by Mauro Guillén And Esteban García-Canal.
        p.   cm.
    ISBN 978-0-07-179811-2 (alk. paper) — ISBN 0-07-179811-0 (alk. paper)
        1. Developing countries—Economic conditions.   2. Lean manufacturing.
    3. Strategic planning.   I. García-Canal, Esteban.   II. Title.
    HC59.7.G823   2013
    658.4'012091724—dc23

                                                                2012033515

McGraw-Hill books are available at special quantity discounts to use as premiums and sales promotions, or for use in corporate training programs. To contact a representative, please e-mail us at bulksales@mcgraw-hill.com.

This book is printed on acid-free paper.

CONTENTS

A Permanent Revolution

WHEN BUSINESS HISTORIANS LOOK BACK AT THE tumultuous past two decades, they are likely to argue that the most earth-shattering events of the time were the bursting of the high-tech bubble at century's end, the global financial collapse that peaked in 2008, the rise of state capitalism in China, and the near (one hopes) unraveling of the Eurozone.

We don't dispute the importance of those events, and we recognize that many of them are still working their way out. But we think something even more profound has been happening in the shadows while the media mostly looked elsewhere: the spectacular growth of globe-spanning businesses in the developing world. As they displace established firms, redistribute world power, and redefine who is in charge, these emerging market multinationals—or EMMs—are going to reshape the global economic order for decades to come.

A dozen years ago, at the end of the twentieth century, few emerging market multinationals had successfully challenged their European, North American, and Japanese counterparts. Long-established brands such as Sony, Gulfstream, and Hewlett-Packard were still golden. The world corporate pecking order was mostly a game of musical chairs among the same two dozen firms. When *Forbes* published its first Global 2000 list in March 2003, no one could have been surprised by the top 10 entries — Citigroup, GE, AIG, and ExxonMobil among them.

Almost 40 percent of the top 2,000 companies were U.S.-based. More than 60 percent of the corporations were headquartered in three countries alone: the United States, Japan, and the United Kingdom.

Forbes' most recent Global 2000 list—in April 2012—tells a radically different story. A third of its top 25 businesses are from nations barely represented in the listing only eight years earlier. China, of course, leads the way, with oil companies and banks; but Brazil's Petrobas and Russia's Gazprom are right in the mix as well.

Break down the world economic order sector by sector, and the list of global leaders from emerging economies (see Table 1) becomes still more impressive. Argentina's Arcor is the largest candy company in the world; Mexico's Bimbo, the largest bakery; Brazil's JBS, the biggest meat company; and Cosan, also Brazil based, the largest biofuels producer. The largest maker of seamless steel tubes? It's Tenaris, down near the bottom of the world in Argentina.

South Korea's Samsung Electronics is now the world's largest consumer electronics firm, and China's BYD is the top manufacturer of nickel-cadmium batteries, a rising leader in ion-lithium batteries, and now challenging the all-electric automobiles market. Brazil's Embraer is the largest regional jet and a leading executive jet maker, and on and on. The list of emerging market firms poised to become number one in their respective industries over the next few years includes Acer from Taiwan in personal computers, TCS and Wipro from India in IT services and outsourcing, Vale from Brazil in mining, and Sinovel from China and Suzlon from India in wind turbines, among others.

Such rankings, though, tell only part of the story. It's equally important to consider what companies these EMMs have replaced at or near the top of the global leaderboard. Bimbo got to the number one spot by outpacing Sara Lee, one of the great conglomerates of the tail end of the twentieth century. Acer and

TABLE 1

Global Leaders from Emerging Economies, by Sector

FIRM	COUNTRY	INDUSTRY	GLOBAL POSITION
Arcor	Argentina	Confectionery	No. 1 in candy
Bimbo	Mexico	Food processing	No. 1 in bread and bakery
JBS	Brazil	Food processing	No. 1 in meat
Modelo	Mexico	Beverages	No. 1 in import beer
Vale	Brazil	Mining	No. 3
Tenaris	Argentina	Steel	No. 1 in seamless tubes
Bharat Forge	India	Metals	No. 2 in forgings
POSCO	South Korea	Steel	No. 4
Cemex	Mexico	Cement	No. 1 in ready-mix concrete
Braskem	Brazil	Bioplastics	No. 1
Acer	Taiwan	Personal computers	No. 2
Lenovo	China	Personal computers	No. 4
BYD	China	Electronics	No. 1 in Ni-Cd batteries
Haier	China	Household appliances	No. 1
Samsung Electronics	South Korea	Consumer electronics	No. 1
Embraer	Brazil	Aircraft	No. 1 in regional jets
Gazprom	Russia	Energy (excluding oil)	No. 1
Cosan	Brazil	Biofuels	No. 1
DP World	Dubai	Port operator	No. 4
Infosys	India	Information services	Top 5
Wipro	India	Outsourcing services	Top 5

Lenovo now outrank Toshiba and Sony in personal computer sales. In regional- and executive-jet sales, Embraer is ahead of such storied names as Gulfstream, British Aerospace, Fokker, and Canada's Bombardier, the world's number two. Samsung outsells Sony, Panasonic, and Philips in consumer electronics. In telecommunications, Mexican-based América Móvil has eaten the lunch of American giants AT&T and Verizon, and right in their own backyard. Cemex is among the top five cement companies in the world and is number one in ready-mix concrete. China's Haier—the best-selling appliance brand in the world—is rapidly closing in on GE, Whirlpool, and Electrolux in household appliance sales. And India's Suzlon along with China's Sinovel have almost caught up with GE Wind and Vestas in wind-power technology. In the rapidly growing field of bioplastics, Brazil's Braskem has surpassed all the leading chemical companies to become the top producer of a vast array of containers made from sugarcane. Its main clients: Chanel, Kimberly-Clark, Johnson & Johnson, Procter & Gamble, Coca-Cola, and Nestlé.

Draw back the camera to look at the broader picture of the developing and emerging world versus the developed one, and you begin to see a macro version of this same story. Between 2008 and 2010—a mere three years—the number of companies from emerging and developing countries included in the Fortune Global 500 increased from 78 to 117. More important, between 2004 and 2009, the number of such firms among the 1,000 largest investors on R&D doubled from 60 to 120. One more set of numbers to digest: In 2010, 29 percent of the 103,786 multinationals in the world were from emerging and developing economies, up from 21 percent in 2000. These emerging market multinationals now account for a whopping 41 percent of new investment crossing borders in the world.[1]

Begins to sound like a trend, doesn't it? But thus far, this is a trend largely unnoticed by those you would expect to be the first ones to climb aboard the bandwagon—the business press and businesspeople always on the prowl for the next big thing, the next sure winner.

Fortune magazine annually surveys business executives to come up with its list of Most Admired Companies in the world. Not surprisingly, U.S. companies dominate the 2012 list, including the top 13 slots. Germany's BMW finished fourteenth to break the American hegemony; and Nestlé, Toyota, VW, Accenture,

Daimler, Honda, and Unilever also made the list from elsewhere in the First World. The Second World? The top 50 for 2012 includes one company from Singapore (Singapore Airlines, number 23, down from 18 the previous year) and one from Korea (Samsung, number 34, up from 38). And that's it for the emerging markets.

Expand the net out to the top 350 most admired companies, and you'll find no mention of Taiwan's Acer or China's Lenovo (numbers two and four in global market share among personal computer brands), Brazil's Embraer (tops in regional jets), Mexico's Bimbo (tops in bread and bakery), and so on. América Móvil does claw its way into the top 350, but one suspects only because Carlos Slim, presumably the world's richest person, controls the company.

Another example: The number one ranked company in Bloomberg Businessweek's 2010 Tech 100 list was the Chinese battery and electric automaker BYD. For the year, this high-flying emerging market multinational tallied $5.8 billion in revenues, 50 percent higher than the previous year, and operating income of $713 million. Shareholder return equaled a dazzling 246 percent. Number 98 on the list, and the lowest ranked U.S. company to make the top 100, was VMWare, a California-based virtualization software outfit. VMWare's numbers for the year were certainly impressive: $2 billion in revenues, 8 percent revenue growth, operating income of $219 million, and shareholder return of 136 percent. Still, it's easy to see why Warren Buffett took a 10 percent stake in the Chinese company, not the California one.

In fact, one would think that Buffett's interest alone would be enough to turn BYD into a media darling, even if its performance since 2010 has been far more down to earth. Not so. A March 2012 search of the previous 12 months of the *New York Times* turned up exactly one mention of the company: an auto reviewer's complaint that BYD's F3DM electric car was bland,

bland, bland. VMWare, meanwhile, logged almost 1,100 search results for the same time frame. Nothing against VMWare. It's an exciting company, but someone is missing the boat.

We are neither seers nor sorcerers, but even without a crystal ball we are confident in predicting that when *Fortune* publishes its Most Admired Companies 10 years from now, more than a few emerging market multinationals—including BYD—will have muscled their way into the top 50, and they will be dotted heavily throughout the larger list of 350. In business, admiration migrates toward success, and today success is migrating heavily in the direction of emerging markets.

What Is an EMM?

Our working definition of an emerging market multinational has two components:

- First, it's a firm from an emerging market. Emerging markets are those that are growing economically but not necessarily demographically—China and Russia being examples of the latter—but do not have fully developed institutions such as stock markets, labor markets, intellectual property protections, and legal systems.
- But note that not every firm from an emerging market is necessarily an EMM. To be a multinational, a firm must have assets and employees located outside of its home country. Some EMMs have a presence in just one foreign country and others in many countries, but all aspire globally.

As the earlier list illustrates, EMMs are scattered around the world, but they are most heavily concentrated in Latin America, the Middle East, and South, Central, and East Asia. EMMs are also in no way industry-specific. They can be found in heavy industries and light ones, high-tech and low-tech, extraction and information services. Emerging market multinationals do, however, tend to have certain common characteristics:

- They are often closer than old-line firms to their foundational figures and stories. Every company has them—the cutthroat who bribed railroads and cheated his competitors to launch an empire (think John D. Rockefeller and Standard Oil, progenitor to today's ExxonMobil), the manufacturing visionary and social eugenicist (Henry Ford, who later succumbed to virulent anti-Semitism)—but the older the firm and the greater its success over the years, the more buried the original inspiration tends to be. That's not the case with most EMMs. At Haier, many workers still remember the day CEO Zhang Ruimin took a sledgehammer and began destroying a defective batch of refrigerators that his line-workers had produced. At India-based Infosys, N.R. Narayana Murthy, founder and chairman emeritus, still walks the halls, articulating an evolving vision.
- EMMs are also less tied than traditional multinationals to the often crippling effects of having to produce short-term results to satisfy impatient financial markets. Big Board firms spend an inordinate amount of time looking over their own shoulders, fearful of displeasing The Street with less-than-stellar quarterly earnings. EMMs tend to have a different perspective. Sometimes, they are shielded from market pressure by powerful state interests (Chinese companies) or spawned by vast family businesses (Tata Consultancy, an offspring of Tata Group, in India). More commonly, they simply have a go-for-broke mentality that stresses long-term results over satisfying analysts' expectations.

- By their very nature, emerging market multinationals are unencumbered by knowledge and experience. Traditional firms are steeped in, well, tradition: their can't-do and must-do lists are long and calcified. EMMs don't realize there is only one right way to reach their goals. Having to play catch-up with the big boys has forced them down unconventional and often very fruitful paths. No one, for example, told Cemex that acquisitions are to be treated like conquered nations, so its executives hit upon the novel idea of milking all the learning and experience they could out of their new "partners" as the company emerged on the global stage.

- EMMs look at the globe truly globally. Of course, old-line multinationals say they do this, and some actually manage to really do so. But when most traditional firms look to expand abroad, they are looking at heart for NLUs—Nations Like Us. The rough-and-tumble of doing business in the emerging world gives them an early case of the hives before they ever touch ground in, say, Caracas or Luanda or, God forbid, Pyongyang. True, a lot of these companies were once educated in the school of hard knocks themselves, but that was decades, maybe centuries ago. EMMs, by contrast, are right on top of their own roots. They know what it's like to battle their way through elephantine bureaucracies and cope with ragtag infrastructures. Their corporate culture is geared toward inventive solutions to intractable problems. Where mainline firms often see nothing but headaches, EMMs see opportunity.

- Emerging market multinationals also frequently have a home-field advantage going for them. Yes, they have to fight a little harder to make space for themselves on the global stage, but government regulators and license issuers back home can be very slow moving, almost to the

point of catalepsy, when competitors try to move into the
domestic marketplace.

How Did We Get Here?

Now that we have field notes to help identify an EMM, we turn
next to what lies behind this phenomenon. Here, there are two
tracks to explore. One involves what might be thought of as
infrastructure issues—physical, human, and imaginative.

- **Physical infrastructure.** Globalization has become a
  two-way street: improvements in transportation, communication, and other enabling technologies coupled with
  the enormous economic growth of emerging economies
  has transformed the way and the location where goods
  and services are produced and sold. China is no longer
  the manufacturing hub for cheap products, and India has
  moved well beyond low-end IT services. These are now
  economies with technologically sophisticated pockets of
  excellence. Yes, they continue to grapple with infrastructure failures and shortcomings, but some of the most
  exciting innovations in advanced fields such as electric
  automobiles and wind turbines are now coming from
  China and India.
- **Intellectual infrastructure.** Earth to the developed world:
  managerial talent was never the exclusive province of
  today's most advanced countries. Remember that the
  first handbook of strategy, *The Art of War*, was written in
  China about 600 BC. But while successful entrepreneurs
  and seasoned managers have always populated emerging economies, today their numbers are growing by leaps
  and bounds. Emerging market managers attend the best
  business schools around the world, learning not only

accounting and people management but also about market opportunities. Just look at the data for some of the leading graduate business programs in the United States. At the University of Pennsylvania's Wharton School, 37 percent of students in the class of 2012 were international, including 19 percent from Asia and 6 percent from Latin America and the Caribbean. Harvard's MBA program for the same year had 34 percent international students; Stanford, 32 percent. Once, many of these entering international students would have had their sights set on professional careers in the developed world, with mainline, brand-name businesses. More and more, though, these best-and-brightest graduate business students are looking to head back home, to emerging multinationals that are rethinking the way global business can and should be done. Having learned the best ideas from the United States, Europe, and Japan, they intend to combine them with their own business traditions as they help batter down the doors of the old order. In these pages, in fact, you will meet multiple EMM entrepreneurs who have done just that—bold CEOs like Maurício Botelho, Zhang Ruimin, and Tulsi Tanti. If the names don't ring a bell, you are not sufficiently aware of what's brewing in the world of business.

- **Imaginative infrastructure.** Another way to put this is mimetism, from the Greek *mimos* and the Latin *mimus*, to mimic or imitate. Is it a stretch to label this "infrastructure"? We don't think so. Highways show you the way to get where you need to go. Bridges assure you that you can make it over the rivers and canyons that stand in your way. So it is with imagination. The most gifted among us can see possibilities with no path to achieve them, but most of us need something tangible to anchor our dreams on. That's what the cumulative success of EMMs is achieving. Each new success story shows other emerging market companies—and, critically, their founders and executives—that they too can make it to the top.

Infrastructure alone, though, doesn't explain the *why* of the EMM phenomenon any more than the existence of a ladder explains why someone chose to climb to an otherwise inaccessible perch. For that, we have to look—and we do in this book—at broader issues of economic growth, demography, and political upheaval. Let us recap here briefly the circumstances that are enabling emerging market multinationals to take over the world:

- First, emerging economies are growing much faster on average than developed ones. The International Monetary Fund estimates that in the next three or four years alone, emerging economies will grow at an annual rate of 8 to 10 percent, while the developed economies will languish at around 2 percent. Not only are EMMs more familiar with emerging markets than established multinationals and better able to talk their language, they are also closer to the ground where the greatest growth is occurring. EMMs like China's Haier and South Korea's Samsung are using this robust economic growth in their home market to provide a sound base for international expansion.
- Another key trend has to do with demography. With the notable exceptions of Russia and China, emerging economies are growing both economically *and* demographically. Thus, a new and growing middle class of consumers and workers is shaping up in key countries such as Brazil, India, Egypt, and South Africa. Demographic growth poses challenges, to be sure, including the potential for political instability, but it is also a sign of vitality and dynamism. What's more, coupling efficient production at low cost with rapidly expanding domestic consumer

11

markets is simply a winning combination. Companies like Bimbo of Mexico and Natura Cosméticos of Brazil would have bright futures even if they had never ventured beyond their home borders.

- A third momentous trend has to do with political change. More countries than ever have adopted democratic forms of government, but many of the political regimes in the fastest-growing economies are fragile and complex. Companies from the developed world continue to face difficulties dealing with democratic governments subject to multiple pressures from stakeholders, while emerging market multinationals are accustomed to coping with governments and institutional environments in which the rules of the game are malleable at best, and often made up on the fly. Acer of Taiwan has been able to cope with the chaos of emerging markets much better than any developed-country firm, while Egypt's Orascom Telecom has found success where not even the slightest signs of democratic institutions can be found: Orascom is perhaps the only successful foreign firm in North Korea.

- One more "why" to point out: The very weaknesses of many developing countries have proven to be hidden strengths. Infrastructure deficits in emerging economies, for example, have created huge domestic growth opportunities. China was plagued for decades by the absence of adequate transportation networks across its vast expanse. But according to KPMG, China's expressway network has been expanding at a 20 percent annual rate since 2000 and is now the second largest in the world. Similarly, China's central planners are building up the nation's stock of vast, ocean-going, dry-bulk freighters, which means work for not only shipyards but also steel mills and everywhere in between. India's productivity has long been compromised by such basic challenges as securing reliable electricity, so industrial entrepreneurs began to supply their own and in the process sometimes discovered whole new fields of endeavor. Suzlon was a textile business until its founder decided to confront the electricity issue head on; today it is a leader in generating energy from wind. Meanwhile, the execution capabilities developed by local firms at home have proved to be a solid basis for launching international expansion.

Here to Stay

Understand: EMMs are not a flash in the pan. Nor will their ascendancy disappear if and when the world economy finally rights itself. They have built their capabilities to such an extent that they are here to stay. Their moment arrived once emerging economies sustained growth for two decades or more. An expanded domestic market gave them a foundation for global growth. They could allocate more resources to training workers and developing capabilities, and eventually to acquisitions that served as stepping-stones on to a larger stage.

Simultaneously, the world was changing in ways that tended to reward an EMM skill set. Unlike the traditional multinational firms from Europe, the United States, or Japan, emerging market multinationals started their international expansion lacking proprietary technology and strong brand reputations, so they had to compete with different weapons. Unlike McDonald's, Siemens, and Matsushita, they did not wait to expand abroad until they felt everything was under control. Scarcity of resources such as capital or skilled labor invited emerging market multinationals to innovate, to make it possible to accomplish more with less. They turned their disadvantages into advantages.

Today, emerging market multinationals are adapting much faster as populations get older, autocratic regimes are toppled, governments come and go, failed states proliferate, environmental disasters become more frequent and intractable, and technology grows more complex. What began as a necessity—a kind of guerilla-business warfare against the corporate superpowers—has now evolved into best practices and is on its way to becoming what everyone needs to know.

Simply put, down is up. The weak have become strong. In a business world bursting with tectonic shifts—a global economy that won't wait for the ideal product, the best strategy, or the most appropriate implementation plan—street smarts have pulled even with MBA smarts. Today, it's not who you know or what you know or where you learned it but how quickly you can adapt to market, economic, and geopolitical conditions that change with almost unbelievable speed. For businesses and individuals, the path to success has far less to do with the well-blazed trails of the past than with the snap decision making and constant risk taking of virtual-reality death games.

The playing field, in short, has been leveled—even arguably tipped in the emerging markets' favor—and any old-order executive who is sitting in a corner office waiting for the tide to turn and the world to come to its senses is in dangerous denial. A permanent revolution is underway, one that has been building for more than a decade and is now breaking into the open for anyone willing to see. All across the board, in industry after industry, multinational firms from emerging markets are challenging well-established companies, forcing them to redefine their strategies, restructure their organizations, rethink their offerings, and reengineer their business processes.

Lessons from the Trenches

Telling the remarkable story of these new global powers is a key goal of *Emerging Markets Rule,* but there's a parallel purpose, equally as important: limning the lessons of this global phenomenon.

From various perches—the Wharton School, Spain's University of Oviedo, visiting professorships in Argentina and Mexico, membership in the World Economic Forum's Global Agenda Council on Emerging Multinationals—and through multiple articles, several books, and extensive consulting with many of the businesses and top executives we write about in these pages, we have been studying EMMs for more than two decades. We've watched them, as a group, grow from a mere ripple on the global pond to what is quickly becoming a tidal wave, and we have also been able to compare them, over many years, with the traditional firms that they are threatening for leadership and often replacing. Maybe best of all, we have been allowed, through our teaching, to see this unfolding through the eyes of the next generation of global business leaders.

What have we learned? Let's cut to the bottom line: many of the principles of global competition in the twenty-first century are far different from those still enshrined as received wisdom at leading business schools all across the developed world. Winning is no longer simply about inventing gadgets, creating brand equity, and designing the best organizational structure. The new rules are built for speed and designed for maximum flexibility. Critically, too, they have all been extensively field tested in the only place that ultimately matters: the maelstrom of the permanent market revolution that is all around us.

We sum all this up in seven chapters built around the new axioms of global competition:

- Execute, strategize, and then execute again.
- Cater to the niches.
- Scale to win.
- Embrace chaos.
- Acquire smart.

- Expand with abandon.
- No sacred cows!

And then in the final chapter, we leave you with an action agenda. Now, let's get started.

Execute, Strategize, Then Execute Again

Winners act while losers agonize over what to do.

However beautiful the strategy, you should occasionally look at the results.

—WINSTON CHURCHILL

FORMULATING A STRATEGIC STATEMENT HAS BECOME A corporate ritual, a way to keep bad spirits at bay. Stakeholders have grown to expect a clear and workable strategy emanating from the top of the corporation. Customers and suppliers, employees, and—most important—shareholders and bondholders demand proof that top management knows what it's doing in the form of a strategy. Strategies are supposed to give each department, unit, and individual throughout the organization a sense of direction and a path to achieving good performance, financial or otherwise. And sometimes strategies are indeed beautiful, especially when they contain the attributes that we expect to find in business leaders: vision, boldness, and grandiosity.

But strategy making can and does become an obsession. Too often, American, European, and Japanese multinationals suffer from a new type of corporate malaise—too *much* strategizing. Top managers agonize over how to formulate the perfect strategy, and when they hit upon one that captures their imagination, they get infatuated with it. Even worse, when they see performance declining, they tend to focus on changing the strategy instead of honing in on what is likely the real culprit—execution.

In his best-selling book, *From Good to Great*, Jim Collins concludes that "there is absolutely no evidence that the good-to-great companies invested more time and energy in strategy development and long-range planning."[1] Indeed, in company after company, Collins found that the same strategy could lead to very different results depending on who the managers were and how they exercised leadership.

So why do executives spend so much time worrying about strategy? Why do they enjoy strategy making so much? For starters, strategizing is a good method for escaping from the nitty-gritty aspects of reality. It can even become a form of day-dreaming. Execution is simply not the kind of task that the top brass finds attractive or worthy of its time. Unlike strategizing, execution requires attention to detail, precision, and constancy. Little surprise, then, that managers at so many established firms favor delegating the many nuisances involved in execution. They prefer to do the big thinking while other, often lesser paid employees are told to worry about the day-to-day.

In reality, CEOs should be deeply engaged in execution, or else change their title. Strategy determines where a business wants to go, but execution is the art of getting there. Execution means being prepared to put in practice a value proposition aimed at doing well what is good for customers—delivering products and/ or services efficiently and on time. Clearly, the winning approach involves executing *before* strategizing. Benetton and Matsushita are ready examples of companies with strategizing run amok.

Benetton, the Italian fashion firm once admired for its color-ful sweaters and global reach, has tried at least six strategies for cracking the American market over the past decade. Management first tried exports from Italy, which turned out to be too expensive because of high manufacturing and transportation costs, and simply not in tune with consumer preferences across the ocean. Try as Benetton might, most American males simply won't buy brightly colored sweaters.

Next, the company tweaked the designs and the distribution channels, also to no avail. Then they brought in provocative billboard ads from Europe, featuring worthy causes like preventing AIDS or improving race relations, and Americans found them offensive or a naked attempt to exploit sensibilities for profit. Still later, Benetton enlisted Sears and a South Korean manufacturer in a joint venture that fell apart in the wake of the backlash against some of the controversial posters. Most recently, management has made an attempt to imitate competitors by opening megastores.

There was nothing intrinsically wrong with any of these various strategies, but the fact remains that none of them boosted the company's fortunes in the U.S. market, the world's largest. And here's why: top management disengaged itself from *execution*, did not follow up on details, and did not help middle management fully grasp the positive and negative feedback loops of each new strategy. They thought that their job was done once the strategizing was completed.

"The United States is very competitive and requires a specific strategy," argued Vice President Alessandro Benetton in 2010, after 20 years of losses in the American clothing market. "We are considering some alternative in terms of a specific plan for the United States."[2] But while Benetton trots out new schemes, hoping to experience a strategic epiphany, brands like H&M and Zara have surged ahead. The value of their brands now exceeds Benetton's many times over.

Another example of a business that tragically neglected to emphasize execution: once upon a time people praised

Matsushita's 250-year strategic plan. It was visionary, audacious, even epic, and it seemed to set the company on a path toward unending domestic and international growth, catapulted by the wonders of its powerful brands: Panasonic, Technics, and JVC. Such an ambitious plan certainly motivated employees by infusing their daily routines with purpose and meaning. Perhaps, then, the Japanese consumer electronics and electrical appliances giant—now known as Panasonic—should be admired for an unwavering belief in long-range planning and grand strategizing. But is it really wise to make decisions today that could tie up resources into the distant mists of time, especially in a rapidly changing global economy? To be fair, the company founder's faith in far-sighted planning was matched by a compulsive attention to detailed implementation and execution on the factory floor, where humans and machines transformed raw materials into products with mass appeal. Konosuke Matsushita instilled in his employees the values of precision and perfection. What's more, Panasonic offered a unique value proposition: products of high quality at an affordable price.

But American and European observers and managers took note of the company's strategy and long-range planning rather than of its more mundane capability to implement and execute, with dire consequences for many of Panasonic's Western rivals. Thus, Phillips and the now-defunct AEG spent years trying to come up with a long-term strategy for success in consumer electronics and household appliances, without focusing on what really made Panasonic work: operational excellence. European and American appliance makers failed to match the Japanese zeal for manufacturing excellence.

In time, too, the Japanese company forgot its own formula for success. Managerial turnover at the top, embarrassing product quality problems, and a rapid decay in design and marketing capabilities made Panasonic vulnerable to new competitors, and its market share and financial performance plummeted at the hands of South Korean and Chinese electronics and appliance companies. But make a note of why this happened, frame it, and hang it on the wall behind your desk: the issue wasn't that Panasonic had long forgotten its 250-year strategic plan. Rather, it lost ground in the marketplace because it failed to implement and execute with the passion that made it one of the greatest companies of the twentieth century. Top management was, well, sitting complacently at the top, unlike the founder's team of decades past, who spent most of their time on the factory floor and visiting retail outlets, constantly looking for ways to improve both products and operations. Panasonic executives simply forgot the lesson that execution is everything. Strategy formulation needs to be preceded and followed by execution.

The fact is, mundane execution has become much more important than strategizing in the fast-changing global economy of the twenty-first century. Most companies that call for a strategic reorientation of their business are really trying to cope with impending disaster as other companies that are better executors eat market share away from them. Strategizing can also lead to blind alleys. When companies define a market or a product as strategic, what they are frequently thinking is "We are going to lose money, but we really want to keep on trying." Thus, grand strategies often lock companies into a path toward competitive decline. The very rigidity of such plans chokes creativity and limits growth in new areas.

Don't get us wrong: there is a place for strategy in the corporation, but it should not come at the expense of execution. Top management needs to pay attention to both, without delegating the latter. Critically, many of the best strategies are emergent—that is, rooted in practice instead of imposed from above. Innovation in new products and in new ways of making and selling them involves experimentation. Corporations learn by doing, formulating and adapting their strategies as they go.

Strategy should not precede and supersede execution, especially when uncertainty is rampant. In this unstable and uncertain global economy, execute first, *then* strategize based on what you learn along the way. *Spending months or years formulating what you believe might be the best strategy is a self-defeating exercise in a world that changes so fast and is mired in the unexpected.*

While multinationals in the developed world have been busy strategizing, nimbler emerging market firms have been executing their way into leadership positions in industries as diverse as bakery, aircraft, and IT services. No obvious commonalities exist across these three very different types of businesses. The one key thread running through them is precisely the importance of execution for competitive success. The winners from emerging markets did not fall into the trap of overstrategizing because they started out by looking for a low-cost and relatively unsophisticated way to get into the game. Their path to success was by excelling at execution and by adopting a real-time approach to strategy. They came up with winning strategies through learning by doing and experimentation. Their winning sequence could be yours: execute, strategize, then execute again.

You Can Be a Global Baker If You Have the Patience

Let's begin with bread—one of the world's most important staple foods, providing billions of people with a large proportion of the energy and nutrients they need. Bread has contributed to the culture, language, and idiom ("breadwinner," "breaking bread," etc.), and plays a key ceremonial role in several religions. Bread is also a dynamic industry in which innovation and knowledge are relevant to competitive success.

Bread is not only a big business, worth over $400 billion annually, but also one that is becoming more complex and sophisticated as consumers increasingly expect variety and convenience, and lean toward both indulgence and healthy choices. Notwithstanding the fact that rice remains the dominant staple in China and the rest of East Asia, bread is also more and more a global product. Individually wrapped bread-product variants are selling increasingly well in parts of the world where traditional bread has never been able to gain much market purchase.

While the Europeans are the biggest bread eaters, American firms brought modern mass production, distribution, and marketing to the industry, and nobody did it bigger than the Sara Lee Corporation. Once known as the Leading Fresh Bread Brand in America and the Cheesecake Company, Sara Lee was seemingly invincible, and not only in baked goods. The company deployed its marketing prowess across a bewildering array of industries and widely divergent premium brands, including apparel, beverages, coffee, meat, snacks, tobacco, leather goods, personal care, shoe-care products, and even some household items.

By the late 1990s, though, the giant was showing feet of dough. Investors demanded a new strategy, one that would enable the firm to overcome its lackluster performance in the wake of enhanced competition. Sara Lee responded by divesting from "noncore" businesses and focusing on "core" ones, such as food, beverages, and personal-care products, a strategy that few people would take issue with. Yet even this didn't work. In 2001, sales exceeded $17 billion; by 2010, they were down to less than $11 billion, and the company had shed nearly 75 percent of its employees.

What went wrong? The answer is actually fairly simple: the company was not motivated to execute. Too much energy spent thinking about what was core and what wasn't did not solve the far more mundane problem of performance—of making, distributing, and selling bread. Succeeding in the low-margin bread business meant looking for ways to be more efficient in production, nimbler and quicker in distribution, and more persuasive in marketing and sales. Sara Lee executives didn't have the patience for all of that—and they thought that the bread business was not that interesting or core anyway. "Bread is fundamentally a very difficult business," noted Tim Calkins, an analyst for Strong Brands. "It is capital-intensive and very dependent on operational excellence, getting the right amount of bread to the right stores at just the right moment. . . . Faced with a difficult, low-margin and slow-growth business Sara Lee elected to give up and sell it off."[3] The buyer was Bimbo, a Mexican firm that thus consolidated its position as the world's largest bread company, including such iconic products as Thomas English Muffins, Pan Bimbo, and Mrs. Baird's breads.

Bimbo had an entirely different approach. "We're not buying Sara Lee's unit for what it's worth today, but for what it's going to be worth tomorrow," Bimbo CFO Guillermo Quiroz said at the time.[4] In fact, he had good cause to be optimistic.

While Sara Lee had lost its sense of direction and purpose by expanding into too many businesses, Bimbo knew that "focusing on what you can do well" and excelling at execution is crucial. Because executives paid attention first to detail, the company eventually managed to produce, distribute, and market both global and local bread products using 100 efficient local plants, tens of thousands of trucks, and over one million points of sale in 18 countries.[5]

Bimbo once owned flour mills and other factories producing some of its inputs but sold most of them to concentrate its efforts on bread itself. Now Bimbo runs its factories 24/7 in a business that requires speed and precision because of the short shelf life of most bread products. But the company's most significant competitive advantage, the one that sets it apart from other large bakeries, including Sara Lee, is its time-tested methodology for managing a complex distribution network involving tens of thousands of points of sale in each national market. As executives put it, Bimbo's success is all about "a little vision with a lot of planning."[6]

This is a company that does not waste too much time strategizing—worrying about the vision thing. Instead, executives spend most of their time actually running and improving operations, from the baking ovens to the shelf at the small store around the corner.

The company has also developed strong marketing capabilities, including a portfolio of over 150 local brands (including, in the United States, Arnold and Stroehmann's breads, and Entenmann's cakes and pastries), as well as the global Bimbo label. And its global reach means that it can as easily appeal to Hispanics in the United States as well as to Chinese consumers craving Mexican-style foods.

Being a truly global bread company isn't easy. Consumer tastes and dietary needs differ massively from country to country. Brand awareness is also a national issue. People even have distinct preferences as to single- versus multiple-portion packaging. And different cultures eat their bread at different times of the day and together with different types of other foods. In some countries, people love to buy their baguette at the small shop around the corner, while in others large stores are the norm. Competition is tough—you cannot patent a product variant.

Producing the bread on a global scale isn't easy either. Transportation cost and short shelf life require manufacturing close to the customer. Costs for raw materials are on the increase because of climate change, droughts, and the diversion of crops toward biofuels production. In many countries governments regulate the quality and price of staple foods, and protect domestic producers. To top it off, timely distribution to the consumer requires negotiating with truckers' unions and anticipating traffic problems. Note that none of those issues involves strategy per se—they're all about execution. Sara Lee had neither the energy nor the stamina to deal with it all.

In all fairness, bread was probably a business that Sara Lee never should have entered in the first place. Unlike many emerging market companies, Sara Lee executives were under pressure to deliver profitability in the short run. "The bakery division accounts for 20 percent of Sara Lee's revenue, but only 5 percent of consolidated operating income," argued Morningstar analyst Erin Swanson. "We've long believed that the domestic bread business was Sara Lee's Achilles' heel . . . but we weren't convinced the firm would look to dispose of the business when it wasn't firing on all cylinders."[7] Sara Lee eventually gave up rather than make full use of its capabilities in a business it really did not care that much about. As a result of the disposal of the fresh bakery division, "Sara Lee is indeed a simpler, stronger and a better company," commented CEO Marcel Smits. "The bakery business is not the main driver of our profit."[8]

Bimbo is family owned and focused on being a bread-only company, a fundamentally different kind of company from Sara Lee. But its ambition is just as great. In fact, Bimbo is the only bread company with operations on three continents, a predicament that has many advantages. "We know best practices in baking," explained CEO Daniel Servitje, the son of the founder. "We travel around the globe looking closely at all practices in baking plants. We can compare everywhere, and we can detect a good number of opportunities to raise productivity."[9] In a world in which food and water will soon become more scarce and expensive than energy, Bimbo stands to win big.

The company was founded in 1945 in Mexico City by Lorenzo Servitje, an immigrant from Spain. His father had established a cake shop. After opening his own bakery, he partnered with several family members to launch the company with 39 employees and five delivery vehicles, selling four types of bread. Expansion throughout Mexico took place in the 1960s before spreading to Latin America in the 1970s and 1980s. Expansion to the United States was preceded by exports. The company also entered into a joint venture to distribute Sara Lee products in Mexico. In 1996, Bimbo made its first acquisition in the United States, followed by over a dozen others and culminating in the purchases of the U.S. bakery operations of Weston Foods and Sara Lee.

Acquisitions, though, are the lesser part of Bimbo's success story. Any business with sufficient cash or leverage can buy its way into a bigger market share, at least initially. Making the acquired company or distribution channel work better and more efficiently is the real challenge.

"I believe in hard work, humility and leaders who have their ear to the ground and understand the nitty-gritty of their operations and markets," observed Daniel Servitje. "Conditions are constantly changing, so it's very important to keep a firm grip on the day-to-day realities."[10]

From the earliest days of its growth, it seems, the company understood that its distribution system had to run like a Swiss watch. Just-in-time deliveries would reduce the amount of unsold bread returned to the distributors by the retailers, so Bimbo gave them computers—Sara Lee never thought about that. It is hard these days to find CEOs who believe that their job is about truck delivery routes and schedules. Most would much rather spend their time thinking about the next acquisition or the next asset disposal. In the mundane reality of bread making and selling, execution is the cornerstone of profitability.

Bimbo also shows that execution goes beyond efficiency and standardization. The company has learned to differentiate its product offerings by segment and geography. For instance, Bimbo constantly tweaks its recipes to play to the health-conscious consumer. It has eliminated trans fats from all of its offerings worldwide and launched new organic and healthy brands. In China, where growth cannot come from bread loaves, the company focuses on bread-based snacks, wrapped separately. One of the company's best-selling products is *juanqu*, rolled bread with layers of beef floss. "It is similar to steamed *huajuan*, a traditional

Chinese food, but it is still bread," said César Cruz, a Bimbo manager in Beijing.[11]

A key issue with selling fresh bread in China, according to Bimbo executives, is that many consumers equate *fresh* with *living*. Thus, it is necessary to fine-tune the marketing to explain exactly in which ways a packaged food can be considered to be fresh. Bimbo has learned that China's young urban consumers are the most receptive to its products and is planning to expand the market beginning with that socio-demographic group. Another peculiar challenge involves distribution logistics: the company uses tricycles to deliver its products to small outlets located in the older parts of town where streets are too narrow for trucks. Familiarity with large, chaotic urban settings throughout Latin America helped Bimbo respond to these challenges. Here, too, Sara Lee had neither the experience nor the motivation to enter the Chinese bread market.

Just as they are with so many other products, Asia's emerging economies are the new frontier for baked goods. China is fast becoming one of the world's largest markets for them, and growth is driven by both volume and value. India's market is expected to dovetail with China's, and Bimbo is uniquely positioned to take advantage of this growth in both countries, given that the markets are crowded with small competitors ripe for consolidation. But this is an opportunity open only to those willing to deal with intricate and tedious details of execution.

The company's experience in China since it launched its first product in 2007 "has been full of learning, unlearning, experiences, challenges and failures," admitted Jorge Zárate, Bimbo's general manager in China. Some products did not work in the market as planned. "I believe that we still have a long way to go and many things to discover."[12]

Zárate is not shy about Bimbo's goals in the world's soon-to-be largest economy: "Short term is expansion, to deeply understand our clients, [our] consumers, and our competitors, and to develop a local talent [pool]. Medium term is to continue growing and expand as a national brand. In the long term we see China as one of the primary sources of growth for Bimbo Group, as well as a source of innovation and talent to other opportunities."[13] Here we see a strategy wrapped around implementation. You execute to figure out what strategy works, and then you pursue it relentlessly by focusing on execution itself.

Zárate is right: if you can succeed at the improbable task of selling bread-based products in China, you can both leverage product innovations in other markets and redeploy the pool of talented managers that made the impossible happen so that the firm can meet other challenges around the world. Companies often forget that what makes some of them great is not collecting the low-hanging fruit but reaching out to the sky. Thus, Bimbo got the basic sequence right: get down to business, see what works and what doesn't, improve execution, learn as you go, and then strategize by building your company's future on the proven basis of the experience gained. Once you have a strategy, don't forget about following up on the details of execution.

Excelling at Execution Can Turn You into a Global Aircraft Maker

If you think that bread is a difficult industry, consider aircraft manufacturing. Imagine yourself competing in an industry in which every new product launch puts the entire corporation at risk. Moreover, your customers are among the most unpredictable, idiosyncratic, and cash-strapped in the world. One day they place orders for hundreds of millions of dollars, and the next they downsize the contract or cancel it altogether. To make matters even more complicated, airlines are always asking for customized cabin designs, specific engines, and other expensive features. And they have made a habit of placing some orders with you and others with your main competitor, which goes to international court every other year accusing your company of obtaining illegal subsidies, dumping, or worse.

The airlines, of course, are also between a rock and a hard place. They face stiff competition from one another, unpredictable weather, sharp seasonality of demand, irascible passengers who are very price sensitive, strong pilot unions, and rising fuel costs they have no choice but to absorb. It is a business in which most companies teeter around the breakeven point, but few give up. Hence, excess capacity is rampant, and profitability is next to mission impossible. Where airlines win (or at least survive) is by increasing their margins—filling up their planes with as many passengers as possible and turning them around fast, charging additional fees for quality and service, and cutting costs—and better aircraft can help on all three counts. A well-designed, easily serviced jet can carry more passengers and be used for more flights during the same day. Passengers prefer a comfortable, spacious cabin with reduced engine noise. Fuel efficiency and low maintenance costs can make a huge contribution to the airlines' bottom line as well.

Welcome to the wonderful world of aircraft manufacturing, where execution is also key to success. The industry is divided into two main segments. Boeing and Airbus dominate the market for large aircraft with 110 or more seats. The "regional" segment of aircraft with fewer than 110 seats is also a duopoly: Embraer of Brazil and Canada's Bombardier. Long gone are Fairchild Dornier, British Aerospace, and Fokker.

Bombardier was the first manufacturer to respond to the airlines' desire for a regional jet to replace the cramped, noisy, and uncomfortable turboprops used on short commuter routes with high flight frequency. Back in the late 1980s, the Canadians stretched a business jet into a small airliner seating 50 passengers, the CRJ-100. Embraer followed with two new jets specifically for the segment, the ERJ-135 (37 seats) and the ERJ-145 (50). Both manufacturers eventually sold a thousand-plus units of their new regional jets to Continental Express, American Eagle, and other commuter airlines eager to use smaller planes to avoid union restrictions on the crewing of larger jets. And with that, the regional jet market was born. "Twenty years ago no one could see a jet operating with 50 seats being economically viable," remembered former CEO Maurício Botelho. "Technology developed and today we see thousands of such regional jets."[14]

But while Bombardier and Embraer made the regional-jet market virtually in tandem, the race to the top wouldn't stay tied for long. Bombardier got mired down with quality problems in landing gears and delivery delays. Meanwhile, Embraer was focusing on operational excellence and pulling away from its chief competition. The firm designed low-maintenance jets in anticipation of cost pressures in the airline industry. Next, it designed regional planes, such as the 190 and 195 series, that rivaled their larger counterparts in terms of performance and cabin comfort, while cutting the operational and maintenance costs to the airline.[15]

Within a few years, Embraer had become the darling of both aircraft connoisseurs and airline passengers. In 2001, Botelho won the Aeronautics/Propulsion Laureate Award given annually by *Aviation Week & Space Technology*, the leading aerospace magazine, for "correctly reading the transformation of the commuter airline industry from turboprops to jets—an insight not gleaned by many established European and American manufacturers—and by focusing on a single overarching objective: customer satisfaction."[16]

Airline executives concur. Embraer is "a company that has proved they know how to build airplanes that the market will want," argued David Neeleman, founder of JetBlue Airways. "Thanks to the Embraer 190, combined with our narrow-body fleet, we can enjoy the benefits of wider market coverage and develop greater business opportunities, while offering the same level of comfort to our passengers," said Formula One legend Niki Lauda, founder of Austria's second-largest airline, Niki.[17] Over 80 airlines in more than 50 countries fly Embraer jets.

Given that Embraer was once state-owned, many people dismiss its success as the result of government largesse. But this rapidly emerging multinational has been winning the old-fashioned way: by attaining the best efficiency and delivery ratios in the industry, beating out competitors in Europe and the United States burdened by higher costs and lower operating performance.

As with Bimbo, Embraer's recipe for success is disarmingly simple. Start by focusing on what you can do best along the value chain, invest in training your human resources, then encourage them to make improvements throughout the manufacturing process.[18] One key outcome was to cut assembly times. For instance, Embraer managed to bring down assembly times for its wildly successful ERJ-170 aircraft from 6.5 to 3.6 months.

How did the company actually do it? By adopting Toyota's famous supply-chain principles. For its older 145 series of planes, Embraer relied on 350 suppliers, four of which were risk-sharing partners. For the 170/190 series, the company cut those numbers to just 38 suppliers, of which 16 shared risks, while offering customers flexibility and performance both before and after the sale. Once Embraer fine-tuned this approach, Bombardier started to lose market share, without being capable of improving its own assembly efficiency and in the face of several embarrassing quality problems. Orders poured into Brazil from airlines around the world, including British Airways, Air France, and major American carriers.

Like Bimbo, Embraer also lacked the kind of technological advantage that made Fairchild, Fokker, or Bombardier formidable competitors. As an emerging market company, it had to create the supplier base almost from scratch in a location with few other advantages save for labor cost. The path to success necessarily required outstanding operations and stellar execution. The company started by making relatively simple planes until they could catch up technologically. By then, neither Fairchild nor Fokker were in a position to survive given their higher costs. Bombardier has stayed in the game, but in an increasingly precarious position.

To make sure the company stays on top, Embraer executives have also set up a network of assembly and service operations in China, Europe, and the United States. Embraer established a majority equity joint venture in China in 2002, with two companies controlled by Aviation Industry Corporation of China (Avic). This move was aimed at reducing its dependence on the U.S. market for export sales while simultaneously gaining a foothold in a market projected to grow fast.

Like other multinationals, Embraer took a road into China that was not carpeted with roses. The joint venture's deliveries were plagued by delays due to red tape when it came to securing supplies and obtaining certification for the planes. Production of the relatively antiquated ERJ-145, a 50-seater, came to an end in 2010 after assembling a mere 41 units over a period of seven years. Embraer would have liked to retool the plant to assemble the 190 series, which averages 100 seats, but Avic balked at the idea, fearing competition with its own regional jets.

Embraer's Chinese experience is hardly unique—archrival Bombardier sourced fuselages from China for export but could not sell a single plane domestically in seven years—but the setbacks in China could well be a blessing in disguise, a lesson in executing that is in the short term as important as planes sold.

Indeed, now that it is climbing out of its own adolescence, Embraer's biggest challenge is to anticipate the impact of the new entrants into the regional segment. Mitsubishi of Japan, an exceptionally capable company, plans to mount a major challenge to the established duopoly by 2014 and has reached an agreement with Boeing to jointly offer customer support. Like

Embraer, for the past three years Mitsubishi has been discussing with potential customers even small details such as the overhead luggage compartments.

Russia's Sukhoi and Avic, Embraer's old China partner, are also launching a line of regional planes, but both must deal with some fundamental problems, including shedding bad habits acquired during decades under state central planning. While Embraer also started as a state-owned firm, it was privatized in 1994. That leaves Sukhoi and Avic years behind the Brazilian company when it comes to marketing, customer support, and ramping up production to profitable levels.

Almost stereotypically—given Russia's reputation for building unsafe, uncomfortable, and underperforming aircraft—quality problems beset the first delivery of Sukhoi's 100-seat Superjet to Aeroflot, prompting the airline to ground the plane. "Yes, it is a Russian aircraft," said a spokeswoman for the parent company rather defensively. But "it is made in cooperation with world-leading suppliers," in reference to the French and Italian partners that collaborate with Sukhoi.[19]

For their part, the Chinese have one key advantage over other new entrants in the field: the country is already a vital node in the global supply chain for the aeronautics industry. But the Chinese also face one significant obstacle: they seem to view the regional jet market as a way station on the way to a bold, even visionary strategy aimed at the large-aircraft segment. "The Chinese people must use their own two hands and their wisdom to manufacture internationally competitive large aircraft," declared Prime Minister Wen Jiabao in 2008. "It is the will of the nation and all its people to have a Chinese large aircraft soar into the blue sky."[20]

That's understandable—the Chinese have big dreams in every direction these days. But focusing on the stars is not the best attitude to have when what matters is patient execution and attention to detail. Emerging market firms, it turns out, are not immune to the "strategy thing," especially when government asks them to pursue goals that go beyond the purely commercial to include national status and pride. Note the difference with Embraer: "We will never make a move toward a larger aircraft on pure strategic vision or something like that," asserted CEO Frederico Fleury Curado.[21]

Embraer is one of the most inspiring business stories from emerging economies. "This is the only company in the entire world that has successfully entered the market for building aircraft since 1960," observed airline analyst Richard Aboulafia, "and it's the only company that's entered the jetliner market since World War II for regional aircraft. That's an extraordinary achievement."[22] Stellar execution made Embraer the great company that it is today. It also is a forward-looking company, being the first manufacturer to fly a jet powered by ethanol.

Succeeding in the Brave New World of IT Services

The global IT services business is worth some $300 billion and dominated by companies that took advantage of their position as hardware manufacturers to become IT service providers. Hewlett-Packard, Fujitsu, and Xerox managed that kind of transition while their traditional hardware businesses declined, but IBM has been the one that really excelled in this transition, both as measured against its own American peers and as weighed against a whole slew of upstart, emerging market rivals. IBM's IT services revenue is about $40 billion, while the two emerging market multinationals among the sector's top 15, India's Tata Consultancy Services and Wipro, are merely one-eighth the size of Big Blue.

As uncomplicated as it seems, putting the business model of IT outsourcing into practice is quite demanding. It involves designing, operating, managing, and/or supporting the information and communication systems of clients. These companies also run their clients' business processes, such as logistics, human resources, and customer relationships. Simply put, IT is all about execution. From its inception some 50 years ago, success in the IT sector depended more on labor productivity than on capital requirements—people, not machines, were the crucial factor. Companies had to set up shop next to their clients, and most large clients were in Europe, Japan, or the United States. Emerging markets could well have been located on another planet as far as this industry was concerned.

And then an asteroid struck Earth in the form of the telecommunications revolution, transforming IT services outsourcing beyond recognition and dissolving many of the traditional competitive advantages of the incumbent players from Europe and the United States while placing emerging market companies in the middle of the playing field. Emerging economies became relevant because of their lower costs and the new possibilities offered by the new telecommunications technologies. A software engineer halfway around the globe from the client could work on a customized service application while the system was down for maintenance overnight. Even better, a team of engineers with different kinds of expertise and located in different parts of the world could now collaborate in real time to offer clients a customized and integrated solution. This momentous change forced existing players to start behaving as if they were companies from emerging economies—or else go into extinction. It was a tough fight because emerging market firms already had their feet on the ground and knew how to exploit their newly acquired opportunity around the world.

No wonder IT outsourcing became *the* business craze of the day, shifting the boundaries of the corporation, embedding it in global networks, and catapulting some emerging economies like India's to global celebrity. The corporate world had already seen the outsourcing of blue-collar jobs; now white-collar occupations were also subject to a similar delocalization, driven by the lower costs for expert labor in emerging economies. Companies learned that their value chain could be diced and sliced years before Wall Street started to apply a similar recipe to subprime mortgages.

It was in this primeval soup of rapidly changing technologies, corporations hungry for cost cutting, and large pools of skilled engineers and other experts that Tata Consultancy Systems, Wipro, and Infosys started to make a name for themselves.

Consider the example of Infosys, the second largest of the three in terms of number of employees and the value of IT services exported. It was founded in 1981 by N. R. Narayana Murthy and six engineers in Pune, India, with just $250 of startup capital. The company rapidly moved to Bangalore in search of a more munificent environment for IT services. Step-by-step, Infosys improved its client base, opened an international office in Boston, and started to build a competitive advantage based not only on wage differentials but also on quality. During the 1990s, Infosys realized the importance of providing end-to-end services to its clients instead of accepting jobs involving subsystems of IT. This move implied being able to not just undertake labor-intensive projects but also reengineer entire internal processes of its clients at the least-possible cost. A daunting challenge to be sure for this young, small, and relatively inexperienced Indian firm when compared with the large corporations whose systems it was expected to overhaul, streamline, and optimize.

In order to win customers, Infosys had to make its program-mers be available 24/7—close enough to them to understand their needs while still able to match the expertise and efficiency levels of other providers around the world. To meet this chal-lenge, Infosys adopted a self-styled Global Delivery Model that enabled project managers to locate each task exactly where it could be performed most efficiently. The company also man-aged separately activities that required constant interaction with the client from those that could be undertaken in a "scalable, talent-rich, process driven, technology-based, cost-competitive development centers in countries like India," according to the founder. "The customer gets better value for money because, in a typical project, only about 20 to 25 percent of the effort is added near the customer in the developed world, and 75 to 80 percent of the value is added from countries like India where the cost of software development is lower."[23]

Over the years, Infosys built an infrastructure of 65 offices and 63 development centers in India, the United States, Canada, Australia, Japan, China, the Middle East, the United Kingdom, Germany, France, Switzerland, the Netherlands, Poland, and several other countries. Infosys initially designed this model for software development, then extended it to consulting services more broadly. "We believe that 35 percent of the consulting effort can be done in India, such as proposal preparation, presentation preparation, research, and analytics," said Murthy. "Similarly, in the case of our business process outsourcing organization, equity research for a major European bank can be done in Bangalore. The bank is getting better value for money, and they're able to compress the cycle time."[24]

In many ways, Infosys offers arbitrage. It helps clients tap into different pools of technical skills and capabilities located around the world and offers their services at the lowest possible price and on a timely basis so that cycle times can be shortened for this era of 24/7 global hyper-competition. "The most important ingredient is talent," S. D. Shibulal, CEO and managing director of Infosys, told us at the company's lush, sprawling training campus at Mysore, the largest of 10 facilities in India with capacity to house 14,000 engineers while they undergo training for six months, learning how to get technical jobs done more efficiently.[25]

On the surface, emerging market IT players like Infosys would seem to have almost unassailable advantages over their developed-market competitors. Their entire ethos, after all, has been built around cost-efficient operations, and they are uniquely positioned to use a large pool of relatively low-priced talent coupled with new digital technologies to offer low-cost solutions to clients located worldwide. So do American and European firms even stand a chance? Yes, if they can forget to some extent their own pedigree. No one offers a better example of that than one of the most pedigree-rich firms in the world: IBM.

Big Blue was a technology powerhouse in many ways. It boasted the invention of the ATM, the hard disk drive, the airline reservation system, and the first computer to defeat a world chess champion, to name but a few breakthroughs. It amassed the largest patent portfolio in the industry, and five of its employees won the Nobel Prize. But during the 1980s the world of technology and computing changed faster than IBM itself. By 1993, the once all-powerful company was on the verge of splitting itself into small pieces, given the poor performance of its personal computer division. Despite enjoying a quasi-monopoly position in mainframe computers and having defined the industry standard for personal computers, the open architecture of the IBM PC and the stubborn escalation of commitment to the OS/2 operating system, which failed at becoming an industry standard, made it impossible for the company to compete with a new generation of fiercely entrepreneurial PC companies.

Desperate for a new direction, shareholders demanded that heads roll. A new CEO, Lou Gerstner, was hired from outside the computer industry. He immediately proposed turning the company into a full-range IT services provider, including software, systems design, and consulting.

Here's the important point, though: Gerstner didn't come up with a new strategy drawing on abstract and grandiose ideas. Nothing could be further from the truth. As an outsider, Gerstner immediately realized that IBM was not listening to the customer, was not focused on implementation as opposed to sophisticated products, and was not excelling at execution. His experience in consulting alerted him to the primacy of process and execution. He was also keenly aware of the importance of being customer-centric. Gerstner's insight was radical because it entailed a revolutionary idea for a company like IBM—namely, paying attention to the customer's needs on an individualized basis.

Big Blue had grown to dominate the global computer industry by being a technology leader and by setting the standards for both customers and competitors. In other words, it was a company accustomed to imposing its vision, strategy, and products on buyers. Gerstner proposed to listen to customers and to offer each of them an individualized solution to their entire information-processing needs, years after emerging market firms had pioneered the idea.

IBM's glory days had enabled the company to build a worldwide presence. Its capabilities as a large and integrated multinational corporation were second to none. Gerstner thought IBM could leverage this legacy to help other firms operate globally as effectively and efficiently as his company had in its incarnation as a computer hardware provider. He wanted IBM to help other large corporations make the most of their business operations in the context of the revolutionary changes taking place in the world of information and telecommunications technology. A first important step in realizing the new IBM was to shed divisions that could not contribute to servicing customers by meeting their IT needs. This process of refocusing around software and services initiated by Gerstner eventually led IBM to dispose of the PC business, which was sold to China's Lenovo in 2004 shortly after his departure as CEO. Simultaneously, Gerstner acquired companies to fill in the gaps in IBM's capabilities, including Lotus and Price Waterhouse Coopers' consulting business.

Implementing Gerstner's customer-centric view of the company was far from easy. For a company accustomed for decades to enjoying a monopoly position in the market, adopting a strategy of providing ad hoc integrated solutions for clients required a major turnaround, large-scale mental and behavioral change, and sustained attention to execution. In his memoir, Gerstner wrote that "fixing IBM was all about execution. We had to stop looking for people to blame, stop tweaking the internal structure and systems. I wanted no excuses. I wanted no long-term projects that people could wait for that would somehow produce a magic turnaround. I wanted—IBM needed—an enormous sense of urgency."[26]

The turnaround IBM began under Gerstner is even more remarkable when you look at how its one-time competitors in the computer hardware business have coped with their own diminishing futures. HP, for instance, acquired Compaq in a huge and ultimately failed bet for reviving its presence in the hardware industry. Despite the vast amount of resources pooled in the wake of the HP-Compaq merger, the company was still unable to be as innovative as Apple has been. After years of decline, HP is finally getting out of the business of making computers and trying to gravitate toward IT services. To ease the transition, HP paid astronomical premiums to acquire consulting and software firms such as EDS and Autonomy to make up for lost time, but even that might not be enough. When you're caught in quicksand, thrashing around just makes you sink faster.

IBM could have continued acting like the large, established company that it was, buying and selling businesses hoping that some combination would eventually stick—exactly the strategy HP was eventually forced to pursue. Instead, Gerstner asked his managers to behave like Infosys and other emerging market competitors— like firms, that is, with no other option but to excel at execution. But you can push the emerging market analogy only so far.

After all, IBM already had a global presence and all those Nobel laureates. Infosys had to build its reputation as a global IT services provider from scratch so that it could overcome the natural, initial reluctance of clients to outsource noncore but critical IT activities to an unknown company whose headquarters was thousands of miles away. Clients needed to know that the company was not only technically competent but also trustworthy. That required executing in a different but equally critical way—in building values and reputation.

"I think if you ask me what distinguishes Infosys from many other companies, it is the following: We have a very strong value system," argued Murthy. "In fact, when I address new hires, the main thing I talk to them about is the value system. I tell them that even in the toughest competitive situation, they must never talk ill of customers. For heaven's sake, don't short change anybody. Never ever violate any law of the land."[27]

Here, too, attention to detail has clearly paid off because Infosys is widely admired today for its corporate governance practices and its reputation for honoring its commitments to clients.

Execute, Strategize, Execute

The first business message from emerging markets is loud and clear: stellar execution pays off, whether the industry is a traditional one like baking or is all about high-tech gadgetry like aircraft. As depicted in Figure 1, good execution begins with focusing on what you can do well, putting the customer first, attaining world-class efficiency in your operations, and delivering to the customer on a timely basis. Once you learn how to execute well, *then* you can develop, adapt, or upgrade strategy on the fly, incorporating what you've learned through execution—and proceed to execute again. But by all means, do not strategize without building a strong execution foundation first.

The paired examples of IBM and Infosys, Bombardier and Embraer, and Sara Lee and Bimbo illustrate that a great strategy

FIGURE 1

Execution leads to customer value.

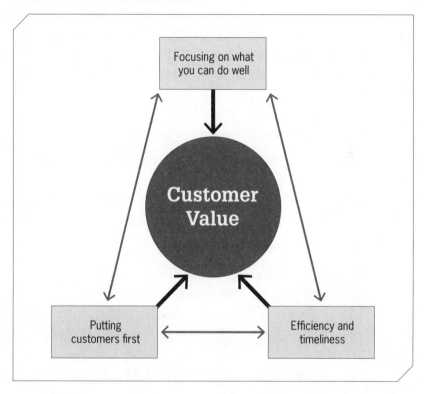

is not enough, and that too much strategizing without attention to execution can wreck a company. Indeed, oftentimes, the best strategies emerge from execution: How can you possibly identify what will work without first seeing it work? Execution is one of the most significant business challenges of our time, especially when so many companies from emerging markets are taking over the world with disarmingly straightforward strategies and simple recipes to achieve success.

Eike Batista, the founder of EBX, the world's fastest-growing mining and energy group, likes to say that X stands for both execution and for multiplying shareholder returns. He likes to remind everyone that he is an engineer, and that execution is what has enabled him to become the world's seventh-wealthiest person.[28] "Execution is really the critical part of a successful strategy," Gerstner wrote in his memoir. "Getting it done, getting it done right, getting it done better than the next person is far more important than dreaming up new visions of the future."[29] Amen.

Cater to the Niches

Follow the path of least resistance.

*Any customer can have a car painted any color
that he wants so long as it is black.*

—HENRY FORD

IN 1909, HENRY FORD PROPOSED A RADICAL IDEA, THE world embraced it, and thus was launched the age of Mass Production and Mass Consumption—*mass* with a capital *M*. Ford made one car—the Model T—in one color, basic black. If you wanted a Ford, that was the choice. And it worked. By paying attention to the mainstream of the market and neglecting the niches, Henry Ford became history's first billionaire.

Unfortunately, many executives today are stuck in a Henry Ford time warp. They continue to believe that only the mainstream mass market is attractive from the point of view of growth potential and profitability. Large, established multinational firms tend not to bother with marginal customers. "Small niches are just not worth the effort," they claim.

But consider how much the world has changed over the past 100 years:

- New technologies in the form of flexible production systems enable companies to produce smaller batches and be profitable. Toyota has made an art of it.

- Selling to a small market segment in just one country may be a losing proposition, but doing so across a large number of national markets can be enormously profitable.
- Most important, niches can be thought of as stepping-stones into the mainstream mass market, especially when entering a foreign country with large, entrenched local competitors.

Companies from emerging markets have perfected the use of market niches, homogeneous groups of customers with unattended needs by the market leaders, as launching pads to global domination. We saw in the last chapter how Embraer used operational excellence to outpace the competition, but the Brazilians also aggressively moved into the overlooked need for regional jets, a niche that industry giants Airbus and Boeing dismissed as a residual market. Now, Embraer is applying the same principles in other well-defined niches, including executive, VIP-transport, and light-training jets; intelligence-surveillance-reconnaissance aircraft; and cargo aircraft.

This is also how Haier of China became the world's largest household appliances brand. Haier's global success started with a timid product launch in a tiny niche segment of the U.S. market, one that established firms didn't even know existed. Modelo, the Mexican brewer, went global similarly, within the niche of light, exotic import beer with its famous Corona Extra label. Natura of Brazil is not yet the largest cosmetics company in the world, but it is growing rapidly by focusing on market niches neglected by huge companies such as L'Oréal and Procter & Gamble.

Incumbent firms tend to look down on an emerging market firm entering a small, underserved niche in their own backyard. They see an annoying gnat, not a Trojan horse using the path of least resistance to take over the stronghold of an established brand. Indeed, often they don't catch on until it's too late. "When I look across the major appliance categories, I've not yet seen [Haier] have any perceivable position," Whirlpool's David L. Swift, the head of the North American Region, told a reporter back in 2006.[1] Within four years, Haier had become the leading brand in the industry. Embraer faced a similar skepticism from the industry's aristocratic establishment. "Years ago our competitors said: 'How dare those ugly ducklings from South America try to sell a jet in the Northern Hemisphere,'" remembered Satoshi Yokota, Embraer's head of engineering and development. "Fortunately, they underestimated us."[2]

Often, too, established companies find niches—and the effort required to reach them—beneath their dignity. L'Oréal, one of the world leaders in personal-care products, always thought that direct sales represented a second-tier market that could tarnish the image of the company and its brands. Delivering catalogs through independent salespeople or organizing sales events in someone's living room simply wasn't what the French company did to sell its products. That is, until Natura showed that approaching the client directly with a quality, even high-end product was a great way to gain market share. Nowadays, given the importance of direct sales in emerging markets, L'Oréal is considering an acquisition specialized in direct selling—tacitly admitting failure.

In many ways, established firms miss the relevance of niches because of deeply ingrained beliefs about the nature of the world. They think globalization equals standardization of tastes, preferences, and needs. They believe that globalization is a tsunami, when it really behaves more like a tornado, bringing about big effects in some specific areas while leaving others unscathed. Customer preferences remain fragmented across countries and among customer groups looking for product differentiation and multiple brand offerings. The fact is, globalization has made niches *more*, not *less*, relevant.

Let's examine how Haier, Modelo, and Natura stunned established firms by growing global out of a niche market.

The World's Leading Household Appliance Brand

The global market for household appliances is big and difficult to crack. We're just too idiosyncratic about what we do within our homes. In some countries, people prefer front-load washing machines, while in others they like to throw their clothes through an opening on the top. Those preferences are further shaped by the intended location for the appliance—under a countertop or in a dedicated laundry room or closet. The size of the freezer in refrigerators needs to be large in countries like the United States, where people shop once a week, as opposed to Europeans, who go to the grocery store around the corner every day. Preferences also differ within national markets: older consumers expect reliability from their household appliances, while younger ones look for special features. The needs of people with no kids differ massively from those with offspring. For a long time, European and American companies dominated this market with extensive portfolios of brands positioned to serve each of these different needs. But the likes of Electrolux, Whirlpool, Frigidaire, and GE bothered to serve only relatively large segments of the market.

Enter Haier, the world's new leading household appliances brand. Its beginnings were inauspicious at best. Imagine a gloomy and decrepit refrigerator factory not far from the workers' living quarters in a dirty part of town. The wooden window frames had been taken down by employees to provide fuel for heating. The scene was chaotic, with tools and equipment scattered everywhere. This is not one of the Victorian-era factories described by Charles Dickens, or one of Karl Marx's "satanic mills." It's the Qingdao General Refrigeration Factory, located in the namesake city on the East China Sea halfway between Beijing and Shanghai. The Qingdao factory was founded in 1955 by a group of workers as a collective enterprise just before the infallible Chairman Mao launched his ambitious, and ill-conceived,

Great Leap Forward, intended to remake China as an industrial power.

The company languished for decades, one of hundreds of minor appliance makers in China. Then, in 1985, seventy-six refrigerators were found to be defective, and Zhang Ruimin, who had been appointed as CEO a few months earlier by the local government, asked the workers to smash them with a sledgehammer. Nobody followed his orders—they would rather repair the faulty appliances and take them home, given that each was worth two years of their wages. Zhang then took aim at the first refrigerator himself, and the astounded workers followed suit. Zhang was charismatic and authoritarian, and well-attuned to American management ideas. He admired Frederick Taylor, Abraham Maslow, and Peter Drucker, and was intent on improving operations, raising quality, acquiring other factories, and saturating the domestic market with over 100,000 points of sale. His ultimate goal was both simple and wildly audacious: to become the world's leading appliance brand.

Technology was at the core of Zhang's plan to turn the company into a producer of high-quality goods, but Haier lacked state-of-the-art capacity. So in 1985, the same year he led the fridge-smashing party, Zhang signed an agreement with Liebherr to license the low-temperature refrigerator technology commonly referred to as four star, which allows for the preservation of foodstuffs between 3 and 12 months. Haier thus became the only Chinese company offering this product in the local market—other Chinese manufacturers made two-star refrigerators that preserved food for up to one month. But Haier wasn't a passive licensee. The company developed its own technological base and capabilities. "First we observe and digest [a new method]," Zhang said, "then we imitate it. In the end, we understand it well enough to design it independently."[3]

Superior technology was not enough to conquer the Middle Kingdom, however, so Haier committed to delivery in no more than 24 hours within 150 kilometers of a point of sale, and that broke the logjam. As the 1990s wore on, customers in the high-growth Chinese economy could not get enough Haier appliances.

In 1991 the company changed its name and brand to Haier—the Chinese transliteration of the second part of the brand name Liebherr—and started to diversify by taking over 18 domestic companies, most of them in the Quindao area, producing an array of electric appliances such as air conditioners, freezers, microwave ovens, and washing machines. Zhang is fond of saying that these companies were "stunned fish," meaning that they had good factories and distribution networks but poor management. Soon after acquiring them, Zhang turned them around in the same way he had reset the original refrigerator factory, by securing new technology through alliances and active learning. Haier then had an ample portfolio of appliances and design capabilities that enabled it to adapt to the specific needs of various customer groups.

The corporate culture nurtured by Zhang and the autonomy granted to each regional subsidiary within China made it possible to put into practice one of the Haier's mottos: "Never say no to the market,"[4] even in bad times. At the end of the 1990s, Chinese consumer spending was rocked by a combination of high unemployment and oversupply of durable goods, but that didn't slow Zhang down. He pushed his managers to attain and maintain high satisfaction levels even among the least significant customers. "No matter how small they are," said Zhang, "they are ours to keep."[5]

A telling example of this philosophy is the case of the washing machine turned vegetable rinser. Haier's technical after-sales service in one region discovered that some washing machines were breaking down because customers used them not only to wash clothes but also to rinse potatoes and vegetables. Instead of blaming customers for misusing its products, Haier designed a specific, dual-use model for that market niche.

Once Haier had become the dominant brand in China, with a commanding 30 percent market share, the company went global, first making appliances for American retailers to sell, then launching its own branded products. The timing was right. China became a member of the World Trade Organization in 2001, and this meant Haier would no longer have the domestic market for itself. The best defense, Zhang decided, was to mount an attack abroad.

Rather than reach for obscure, underserved markets, Haier followed a philosophy of "first the hard, then the easy." Zhang's number one target was the United States, the most competitive market of all. Why? As Zhang put it, "If we can effectively compete in the mature markets with such brand names as GE, Matsushita, and Philips, we can surely take the markets in the developing countries without much effort."[6] (Note how closely this approach echoes the lyrics of the famous song "New York, New York": "If we can make it there, we can make it anywhere.") The key issue, though, was not the market the company chose but rather how Haier attacked the American colossus—not frontally, but one product niche at a time.

Haier also benefited greatly during this critical period from the advice of Michael Jemal, who at the time was in charge of Welbilt, an independent distributor of imported appliances. On his own, Jemal went to China and convinced Haier executives that a market existed for Chinese-branded appliances in the United States. Jemal specifically identified an underserved niche for compact refrigerators among college students and took the idea to Wal-Mart and other retailers, who responded enthusiastically. Haier executives were impressed and decided to grant Jemal exclusive rights for distributing Haier products in the United States. Shortly thereafter, he was asked to become chairman and CEO of the newly created Haier America. Next, the company turned to wine coolers, also sold through channels directly to the relevant niche market. After that, Haier launched

Frog TV, a learning TV set for children, which did not sell well but helped raise brand awareness.

Jemal's approach was disarmingly simple and a thorough revelation of niche thinking. GE, Whirlpool, Maytag, and Frigidaire "can step on us anytime they want," he said in 2001, "because we are so small compared to them in the United States. So we don't look to compete. What we do is try to find our own position."[7] One of those positions included a chest freezer with a pullout drawer, something never seen before in the appliances industry. In fact, this model—with a top part using a conventional lid and a lower section with a pullout drawer for easier access—was designed following a customer suggestion and a tentative blueprint made by Jemal, and the first unit was produced within one day. "Many companies have a lot of ideas," Jemal said. "The reason we have the winning strategy is that we have the speed, the innovation, and the desire to be the best. You can't find another company that can design a product in 17 hours."[8]

Haier, though, did not stop at niche dominance. The company thought of small market segments as stepping-stones in the process of conquering the mainstream of the market by gradually introducing new product lines aimed at covering a wide spectrum of needs. Ten years after the initial assault, Haier sells its entire product range in the United States, many of them built at manufacturing facilities in Camden, South Carolina, to better serve the market on a timely basis.

Haier has followed the same core philosophy to break into other markets around the globe. The company entered the brutal German market with air conditioners. When distributors there proved reluctant to carry the product, Haier arranged for quality control to be undertaken by a European independent laboratory in order to show that its units outperformed some competing German-made products. Step by step, the company introduced products not only in Germany but also elsewhere in Europe, focusing first on the unattended needs in each market.

After setting up a joint venture to manufacture air conditioners in the former Yugoslavia in 2000, the company established its European headquarters in Italy and a year later acquired a refrigerator plant.

In Asia, Haier entered Indonesia first through a joint venture set up in 1996, initially aimed at producing refrigerators. Power shortages and problems with voltage led Haier to design low-consumption refrigerators able to function with variable voltage. Other Asian and Middle Eastern countries followed. In 2002, Haier entered Japan through an alliance with Sanyo with midsize appliances, ideal for typically smaller Japanese homes. Interestingly, Haier has recently acquired Sanyo's refrigeration and washing machine business units from Panasonic, which had purchased them as recently as 2009, turning the Chinese company into the fifth-largest appliance manufacturer in Japan.

Nowadays Haier is a truly global company with a worldwide sales network and 29 manufacturing facilities and 16 industrial parks in the United States, Europe, Asia, the Middle East, and Africa. The company boasts eight research and development centers in the United States, Germany, Japan, and South Korea, and has been the world's best-selling brand of major appliances since 2009. Only Whirlpool and Electrolux, which market their products through numerous brands, have a greater global market share. This is a huge achievement given the company's humble origins.

Haier's unending growth has been a major nightmare for Whirlpool, which continues to hold the lead position in manufacturing household appliances thanks to its commanding market share in the United States and its 2005 acquisition of Maytag. Whirlpool executives, though, know better than most Haier's uncanny ability to find the path of least resistance to meeting customer needs. "We are organized to understand what customers want and to meet those needs, which are sometimes quite differentiated," said Zhang. "Large companies are established and slow moving, and we see an opportunity to compete against them in their home markets by being more customer focused than they are."[9]

Haier has looked into growing in the United States and elsewhere through acquisition. It, too, had been interested in Maytag, and in 2008, the company looked closely at buying GE's appliance division. But Zhang and Haier are patient and confident enough to realize that they can enhance their position as the world's leading brand through hard work and organic growth.

Creating a Global Niche in the Beer Industry

Beer is the world's most popular and probably oldest alcoholic beverage. Our Neolithic ancestors are thought to have started brewing it more than 9,000 years ago, not long after they mastered cereal farming. Written records from ancient Egypt and Mesopotamia detail methods of beer production. Germanic and Celtic tribes later spread the brewing secrets throughout Europe. The industry is both very global—dominated by Anheuser-Busch InBev and SABMiller—and extremely local, with thousands of regional and local brewers catering to some of the smallest market niches you will find in any consumer product category.

According to Euromonitor International, humans consume about 187 billion liters of beer each year. That's a whopping 108 servings of beer annually for each person 15 years old and above, and amounts to nearly 80 percent of total consumption of all alcoholic beverages. China, the United States, Europe, and Latin America are the largest markets, but this is a business with $240 billion in annual sales worldwide.[10]

Brewing is also an industry in which 5 of the top 10 players are emerging market multinationals. In 2008, InBev of Brazil completed the acquisition of Anheuser-Busch and became the global market leader with nearly 19 percent of volume sales, followed by SABMiller, Heineken, and Carlsberg. The rest of the top 10 are made up of three Chinese firms, Grupo Modelo of Mexico, Molson Coors, and Kirin of Japan.

Founded in 1925 and controlled by a coalition of families since the early 1930s, Modelo has only 3 percent of global volume sales, but it has the most successful global "exotic" niche brand of all: Corona Extra. In 2011 Corona Extra was ranked the world's second most valuable beer brand ($3.9 billion), according to Interbrand, closely followed by Heineken ($3.8 billion). The number one spot went to Budweiser ($12.3 billion),[11] but Bud's strength derives mostly from its big market share in the United States and Canada. Corona Extra, by contrast, sells well not just in Mexico but also in the rest of Spanish-speaking Latin America, the United States, Canada, and China.

"There's no mystery about brewing beer. Everyone can do it," said Michael Foley, Heineken's president in 1995. "It's all about imagery, and value perception . . . Beer is all marketing. People don't drink beer; they drink marketing."[12] And Corona—a light golden beer marketed as "la cerveza más fina" (the finest beer)—has clearly beaten the Dutch firm at that.

"The marketing of Corona has been brilliant, whereas the marketing of Heineken has become schizophrenic," wrote Philip Van Munching in *Beer Blast*, a book about the U.S. beer market. "Corona Extra's association with the tropics and being drunk with a lime are indelible images that work."[13] Van Munching, it should be noted, is no innocent bystander in the beer wars: his family was one of Heineken's U.S. importers from the 1930s to the 1990s.

How have the Mexicans managed to create a global brand in an industry in which all the other major players are lucky to succeed in one or maybe two major markets at most? The answer is niche thinking, coupled with market necessities. The Mexican beer market is both large and sophisticated. The conquistadors brought with them European-style brewing techniques. Upon independence from the Spaniards, the industry expanded quickly during the nineteenth century thanks to the construction of the railroad, which facilitated the transportation of cheap malt from the United States. Today, 90 percent of the industry is dominated by two giants, Modelo and Femsa, which was acquired by Heineken in 2010.

After consolidating its position in the Mexican market, Modelo was forced to go international to keep growing. The United States was the obvious choice because of proximity but presented daunting challenges, including entrenched competitors and sophisticated consumers. Export sales across the border during the early 1980s were low because Modelo was forced to redesign its bottle to satisfy a Puerto Rican brewer that had registered the Corona name. In 1985, Modelo finally managed to settle the legal issue and quickly started to sell the Corona Extra brand in its vintage transparent bottle with the characteristic long neck.

But the company had already set the stage for its assault on the U.S. market. In 1979, it signed contracts with two separate importers. The first focused on the states west of the Mississippi and initially targeted college students, some of whom had tasted Corona in Mexico during spring break. Beach parties were the main advertising theme for this niche. The second importer targeted Mexican immigrants by appealing to their nostalgia for the homeland. This dual-pronged approach to the U.S. market enabled Modelo to establish a beachhead in two different demographic niches. Sales ballooned from 1.8 million cases in 1984 to 13.5 million in 1986, behind only Heineken among imported beers.

During the late 1980s both importers stumbled over decisions concerning the choice of local distributors and points of sale, but by 1997, Corona Extra had surpassed Heineken to become the best-selling beer import in the U.S. market. By that time Corona was selling well outside the two original niches of party-going college students and Mexican immigrants. The beer was now positioned as a "vacation in a bottle" and "fun in the sun." Corona Extra's light character and smooth taste were also familiar to a broad swath of American beer drinkers, something that undoubtedly helped expand sales beyond the original base targets. "You just have to have it," the manager of a popular singles bar and restaurant in Washington, D.C.'s Georgetown neighborhood told the *New York Times* in 1999.[14] Pricing was also a key ingredient of success: higher than domestic beers but lower than Heineken's.

Above everything else, Modelo got it right when its marketers decided to position Corona Extra as a premium import beer highlighting a specific lifestyle. The idea was to appeal to young people who wanted to have fun with their friends but did not want to develop a beer belly. "Corona used the parallel of a tropical vacation as an icon of representing that balance of life's priorities," observed Don Mann, director of Mexican brands for Gambrinus Company, one of the two U.S. importers.[15] Serving the beer with a wedge of lime at bars and restaurants also reinforced its exotic origin and enhanced its taste. Competitors have since tried to jump into the same marketing space with brands such as Miller Chill and Bud Light Lime, but with limited success.

The creation of the North American Free Trade Agreement (NAFTA) in 1993 invited firms on both sides of the border to look for new ways to either further infiltrate the other's market or to collaborate. Modelo chose the latter route by forming an alliance with Anheuser-Busch, selling it a 17.7 percent equity stake in exchange for continuing to be its exclusive distributor in the Mexican market. But Modelo also held on to its two exclusive importers for the U.S. market—a good decision since Corona sold in the United States much better than Budweiser and Bud Light did in Mexico, a trend that continues to this day.

As a result of its 2008 acquisition of Anheuser-Busch, InBev today holds a 50.2 percent equity stake in Modelo but has less than half the voting power. For all practical purposes—and despite going public in 1994—the Mexican firm operates as a separate company, the only major family-controlled beer company that remains in an industry once dominated by dynasties. Perhaps that is why, although the Corona brand is truly global, the company has stayed firmly rooted in its home country, where it is absolutely dominant. Modelo's global success has been built solely on exports from its Mexican plants. The company does not own foreign breweries, although it licenses its brands in some markets.

Modelo's global niche strategy has succeeded beyond anyone's imagination. Corona Extra is the number one import beer in China, India, Indonesia, Japan, Thailand, Vietnam, Australia, Bolivia, Chile, Costa Rica, and Canada, as well as the United States; Modelo products are now sold in 170 countries. (True global reach, given that there are only 192 member states in the United Nations!) Thanks to Corona Extra, Mexico is now the world's largest beer-exporting economy, having surpassed two of the most admired beer-producing countries, the Netherlands and Germany.

Entering the Chinese market, the world's largest, didn't prove as difficult as one might think, mainly because local competitors can't offer such a differentiated, unique, and exotic product as Corona Extra. The main points of sale are bars, karaoke rooms, big retailers like Carrefour, and premium outlets. The company targeted white-collar urban males aged 23 to 30. To reach the right people in the right places, Modelo persuaded Anheuser-Busch in late 2006 to distribute Corona Extra in China. Anheuser-Busch was already well established there, with a 5.4 percent market share plus a 27 percent stake in Tsingtao Brewery, China's second largest. With that kind of backing, Corona Extra quickly became the nation's best-selling import beer. Plans now are to use Anheuser-Busch's distribution in Brazil to introduce Corona Extra to the world's third-largest market, after China and the United States, again positioning the brand as a premium beer for young urban professionals. Clearly, this is a company sequencing nicely from niche thinking to strategic partnerships to global dominance.

While it is true that the great recession, which began in 2008, has hit sales of imported beer disproportionately, Modelo has options at its disposal. "Corona is still a unique brand, which reflects a different lifestyle," said CEO Carlos Fernández, who is a great-nephew of one of the company's founders. "And this is not the first time that we've gone through a bump with that brand. I'm very confident we're going to be able to make it grow."[16]

Modelo can make acquisitions, launch new brands, and ride the wave of growth in emerging markets, where it is uniquely well positioned. "One of our goals is we want in the next [several] years to have almost 50 percent of our revenues coming from foreign markets. Today it's 40 percent," said Fernández. "Australia is having very good momentum. I think Asia will be very important for us going forward. Latin America has been really a surprise for us in many ways. Countries such as Chile, Argentina, and Colombia [have shown] double-digit growth."[17]

Finding a Niche in Personal Care Products

We saw in Chapter 1 that emerging market companies have not yet conquered every industry. In IT services, firms like IBM or SAP are still at the top of their game. Personal care offers another example of how American or European firms can hold their ground in the face of stiff competition from emerging economies—or lose that same territory.

Cosmetics, fragrances, and toiletries generate nearly $400 billion in sales annually. It's a huge market, one that will never go away. No matter age, gender, health condition, or even wealth level, people spend a significant share of their income on personal care. Moreover, many products are aspirational. Leonard Lauder, the chairman emeritus of the Estée Lauder Companies, likes to say that lipstick is the most recession-proof consumer product the world has ever seen.

But big, personal care is also a difficult business. The industry is dominated by giants such as Procter & Gamble and L'Oréal, each with about 10 percent global market share. However, fragmentation of tastes and heterogeneity of needs due to climate, biology, and culture, has led to the proliferation of brands and product variations.

Enter Natura Cosméticos, perhaps the most promising challenger in personal-care products from an emerging economy. The company's recipe for success is all about niche thinking. It targets customers concerned with sustainability and reaches them through direct sales. In fact, one of the key sources of heterogeneity in the industry lies in distribution channels. You can find personal care products at department stores, supermarkets, drugstores, health and beauty salons, online . . . and through direct sales by means of representatives exploiting sales opportunities within their personal network. Global trendsetters like L'Oréal and Estée Lauder shun direct sales, but they happen to be a very important distribution channel in emerging and developing economies—precisely where the growth is. Whereas direct sales account for just 3.3 percent of the market in Western Europe and 8.4 percent in North America, in emerging economies the proportion stands at over 20 percent, with Latin America holding the record at a whopping 27.9 percent.

The world leader in direct sales of personal care products is Avon, a company with origins going back to 1886 and nowadays the fifth-largest player in the industry, with a market share of 3.4 percent. Avon's expertise in direct sales has allowed it to sail through the Great Recession, thanks especially to its burgeoning business in emerging markets. The plain truth is that Avon's main advantage when entering a new emerging country is that larger rivals like Procter & Gamble and L'Oréal have neglected direct-sale channels.

Avon, though, appears to have met its match with Natura. Founded in 1969 as a cosmetics laboratory with a single store in São Paulo, the Brazilian firm makes and brands cosmetics, fragrances, and personal hygiene products. The company is number one in Brazil, with a commanding 24 percent share in one of the fastest-growing global markets—and especially in the high end of the market. Avon ranks number three in the same market but competes mainly in the middle and lower segments. Natura also has significant shares in Argentina, Chile, Colombia, Peru, Mexico, as well as operations in France aimed at learning and serving as a platform for further expansion in Europe.

Natura's business model rests on three pillars:

- **An appeal to ecology, sustainability, and social responsibility.** The company started by using natural ingredients in all formulas and increased this commitment by adopting carbon-neutral operations, refill packages, sustainable extraction of ingredients, and recycled and recyclable materials. Natura uses only vegetable oils in its soaps and creams, instead of animal fat and synthetic components. While this approach presently limits the size of the market, potential future growth opportunities are tantalizing. In 2000, with the launching of the Ekos product line, the company turned itself into a leader in sustainability as well, using Brazil's phenomenal biodiversity as the sole source of ingredients. The company has established 19 alliances with indigenous communities in the Amazon basin to source herbal raw materials and vegetable oils. These alliances aim at ensuring active ingredients and other raw materials meet tight sustainability standards along the entire value chain, from manufacturing to packaging.

Managing this network of suppliers is exceedingly complex because it involves "local communities, cooperatives, NGOs, research centers, and governmental agencies," said Marcos Vaz, sustainability director at Natura. "But in the end everybody wins: nature, communities, customers and Natura's consultants [as direct-selling agents are known] . . . because creating wealth for everybody, from towns to forests, is the essence of the Ekos line."[18] According to Cochairman Pedro Passos, "Ekos is the materialization of what we have been striving for, in terms of values—natural active ingredients, awareness and responsibility. Our company is reaffirming its origins."[19]

- **An emphasis on rapid innovation.** Natura is innovative not only in terms of sustainability but also in the speed with which it brings to market new products that take advantage of the rich array of Brazil's natural resources. To accelerate product development and keep costs under control, the company has launched partnerships with scientific institutions in Brazil and abroad, MIT among them. This includes the commercial use of ingredients from Brazilian biodiversity as well as the "sustainable use of natural resources, social biodiversity, eco-design, and environmental indicators."[20] Astonishingly, Natura generates more than 60 percent of turnover from products launched in the prior 24 months.

- **A big bet on direct sales.** Beginning in 1974, Natura has organized an extensive network of 1.2 million independent sales consultants, of which one million are in Brazil. To reduce costs and preserve flexibility, consultants are not employees of the company. However, the company works very closely with them in order to ensure that they advise clients properly regarding which products to buy and how to use them, and follow Natura's principles and values. For instance, the firm wants all customers to know that it recycles printed catalogues. "From the beginning, Natura's consultants always had a more important role than just make sales," said Guilherme Peirão Leal, Natura's cochairman. "They had to be trained to provide customers with a deeper assistance in such a way that they can identify their esthetic needs and indicate to them the most appropriate products. Sales per se shouldn't be the final goal. Through consultants, we aim at turning the selling of our products into inspirational, self-awareness moments, to be involved in social and environmental issues."[21]

Thanks to this three-pronged strategy, the company has achieved a commanding leadership position in Brazil. Some customers value the use of active ingredients from the Amazon rainforest. "Natura's make-up is truly expensive, but some products you can't find in any other brand," one customer told a Bloomberg reporter. Others value the company's commitment to sustainability. "There's confidence in the brand," another customer said, adding, "I like the idea of being ecologically correct."[22] This is basically the same approach tried by the Body Shop, but with far deeper commitment. In the late 1980s, the Body Shop appeared to be similarly embracing the values of corporate social responsibility and sustainability through multiple initiatives around the world. One of the most renowned was an alliance with the Kayapo tribe from the green forest in the Amazon, which supplied the company with nut oil for a specific product line. Part of a wider program called Trade Not Aid, the alliance received wide coverage in the press, positioning the company as both eco-friendly and an ardent promoter of fair trade. Eventually, though, the project severely damaged the image of the Body Shop brand when it became apparent that the entire operation was little more than a publicity stunt. As insufficient as the Body Shop payments were, they also made the Kayapo ineligible for government subsidies and thus forced the tribespeople to engage in additional activities that threatened the rain forest. The Body Shop, which has been part of L'Oréal since 2006, never recovered entirely from the bad press. Natura is almost certainly too close to the ground and sensitive to the situation to make anything like the same mistake.

Natura's strong knowledge and market bases in Brazil represent solid advantages when it comes to future international growth. It's not just the exotic ingredients. Brazil's racial diversity means that the company has had to develop products for each type of skin, hair, and body shape. True, American firms are exposed to similar diversity in their home market, but they have not turned this into a source of competitive advantage. They deal with each ethnic segment separately without thinking about the implications for global growth.

Natura's homegrown advantages certainly proved crucial to its expansion throughout Spanish-speaking Latin America, where direct sales are as important as in Brazil. Mere exporting didn't do the trick: the company had to replicate its entire value proposition, niche orientation, and preferred distribution channel in each foreign market.

Consider Natura's entry into Argentina in 1994. The direct sale model did not work well at first. Turnover among consultants was high until Alessandro Carlucci, Natura's current CEO, was dispatched to overhaul the underperforming operation. In 2001, Natura turned the Argentine financial collapse into an opportunity by not raising prices and appealing to consumers' sustainability values. The Argentine peso had lost two-thirds of its value against the U.S. dollar, reducing purchasing power substantially, especially when it came to buying imported products.

"We looked for ways to reduce costs and put ads in the major magazines stating that we would keep our prices steady for the time being and would change them if and when local salaries were adjusted," explained Carlucci at the time. "The idea was to create a kind of social pact involving suppliers, employees, and customers, showing to the Argentinean market that we were there for good and expected profits in the long run."[23] In fact, this proved to be an extremely effective way of conveying Natura's values to the Argentinean customer. The company presently has 329 employees and 53,000 sales consultants in the country. Natura has achieved similar successes in Chile, Peru, Colombia, and Mexico.

By now, these multiple and varied experiences have made Natura very effective at replicating its direct sales model abroad. "It takes between one and one and a half years to complete the product portfolio in each new country," Erasmo Toledo, director of international operations, told us. "We neither enter with a narrow range of products nor with a wide one. A narrow range is not profitable for our consultants, and a wide range does not allow us to build progressively the brand. So we enter with a basic range of products and gradually enter new ones as we see the acceptance of the products, and train our consultants on how to use them."[24]

Niche-focused global expansion, however, won't work on autopilot. You need to think carefully about national variations. About 70 percent of Natura's products are common across Latin American countries, but being effective across different geographies requires tweaking. To facilitate building the brand as well as coordinating the consultants, Natura established a few exhibition centers called Casas Natura in selected locations, mostly exclusive commercial locations in big cities. In these centers consultants receive training and customers can try the products, although they cannot buy them. In Mexico, Natura put in place a multilevel system of consultants, with only the top-tier being able to buy products directly from Natura. The company decided to make this adjustment because multilevel direct sales systems were common in Mexico, although Natura made sure that consultants across all levels complied with its values.

France is Natura's only foray outside Latin America to date. In this market, they sell through stores and the Internet as well as via 3,000 consultants. The company views France as a learning lab and launching pad for the rest of Europe. Meanwhile, there are huge growth prospects to exploit back in Brazil. According to *Euromonitor*, Brazil is the third-largest market in the world for personal-care products, behind the United States and Japan, and ranks as the most important in direct sales. The firm, however, stands to win from global sustainability trends once it feels ready to do so. Meanwhile, Avon, Procter & Gamble, and other leading companies are in a bind. None of them has the powerful combination of niche thinking, sustainability focus, and direct-sale experience that Natura possesses.

Following the Path of Least Resistance to Global Success

The success of emerging market multinationals such as Haier, Modelo, and Natura shows that global markets are an amalgam of heterogeneous niche segments in which a variety of strategies can be profitable. Niches, after all, are specific customer groups in which products or services enjoy tribal acceptance. When well managed, niches can become retinues of fanatic followers whose raw enthusiasm can level the playing field when it comes to taking on established firms with greater technological and marketing capabilities.

In today's hypercompetitive global economy, established multinationals need to pay attention to marginal niches for both offensive and defensive reasons. Turning your back on niches courts losing important expansion opportunities outside the home country. Whereas L'Oréal encounters difficulties in emerging markets, Natura and Avon are thriving in them thanks to their expertise in direct sales. Recently L'Oréal considered the possibility of acquiring Avon or another direct seller, although it backed down after assessing the thorny integration issues.

Neglecting niches also can lock your company out of ill-defined but slowly emerging broad markets. Examples of this pattern abound. Back in the 1990s, General Motors enjoyed a technological lead in developing electric vehicles, but top management and the board thought that launching such a product would be disruptive to corporate growth and unprofitable given its limited, niche appeal. Wrong call: most automotive analysts expect hybrids to become much more than a niche in the near future, a trend that will benefit companies like Toyota, which never gave up.

Shifting consumer demographics also turn niches into large markets. Two decades ago, clothing companies ignored the 65-plus age niche. Today, they can no longer afford to do so. Within two decades, it will be the dominant segment in Europe, Japan, South Korea, and China—half of the global economy! Publishers of scientific books and journals grasped the new opportunities in digital technology while trade publishers did not. They thought it would remain a niche market for a long time—and were caught way off guard by consumers' thirst for iPads, Kindles, and Nooks.

Underserved niches provide new opportunities for making profits, but they also represent weak points in the company's defensive perimeter against the attacks of new multinational firms, especially those from emerging markets. For the underdogs and outsiders, market niches are important not only per se but also as points of entry into the mainstream of the market when a frontal attack is not possible. For these firms, following the path of least resistance by targeting niches does not necessarily entail addressing the same segment customers or introducing the same types of products. Niche companies do not always pursue the same niche across markets. Some niche-oriented firms from

FIGURE 2

Choosing the niche approach that fits your company.

emerging markets are perhaps better thought of as discriminators because they offer in each country a specific product-segment combination adapted to the needs of local customers. Thus, there isn't one but two different types of niche strategies:

- The discriminator focuses on a different niche in each country without integrating operations across markets. Haier started its long march to global supremacy in this way.
- Global niche players target the same niche of the market across countries. Natura and Modelo followed this path to success.

Later in the process of expansion, the legitimate aspiration to global leadership invites both discriminators and global niche players to move into the mainstream of the market. Haier is now in the process of making this transition (see Figure 2). But keep in mind that timing is everything. Discriminators and global niche companies cannot afford to move into the mainstream too early—or too late. It's a fine balance that we explore in subsequent chapters.

Scale to Win

How else can you conquer the world?

More steel rails more bicycles more spools of thread more armorplate for battleships more bedpans more barbedwire more needles more lightningrods more ballbearings more dollarbills . . .

—JOHN DOS PASSOS

HE GREAT AMERICAN WRITER JOHN DOS PASSOS described better than anyone the unpunctuated, seamless flow of production that characterized the industrial age of Andrew Carnegie, Frederick Taylor, and Henry Ford. The immense possibilities offered by economies of scale intoxicated the minds of politicians, social reformers, and business leaders alike. Engineers and efficiency whizzes became the most sought-after experts of the day. They ushered in the period of American industrial supremacy that started around 1913 with the first moving assembly line and lasted until the oil shock of the 1970s. The global market was turned into a mass-consumption playground.

Reportedly, President Franklin Roosevelt once said that if he could give every Russian a single American book, it would be the Sears Roebuck catalog.[1] He could, of course, have chosen the Federalist Papers or the U.S. Constitution itself, but in his view neither conveyed what America was all about better than the imagery of large-scale production and mass consumption.

Fast-forward to the early twenty-first century. American and European mass producers have handed over the baton to the emerging market multinationals—and they are building ever-bigger factories and running production lines faster than anyone else. *Citius, altius, fortius.* Most executives nowadays recognize that gaining scale before your competitors do is essential to sustain your position in rapidly growing industries such as electronics, telecommunications, and wind power. Few realize, however, that gaining scale fast can also lock in your leadership position in traditional industries such as confectionery or beverages. Ramping up scale enabled companies as diverse as Samsung Electronics, Arcor, and Suzlon to enter the global big leagues.

Consider the following often-forgotten aspects:

- Few industries are oblivious to the trend toward greater scale. Even firms engaged in craft production of highly differentiated luxury goods have found ways of capitalizing on scale by enlarging their target customer base without reducing exclusivity.
- Scale used to come at the expense of quality and customization—until the Japanese invented lean production and mass customization. Toyota surprised the world by simultaneously slashing costs, reducing quality defects, and offering product differentiation. And until the company was lured into complacency, leading to the infamous accelerator fiasco, its automobiles were the most durable and fetched the highest resale value.
- Flexible manufacturing and widespread outsourcing have made building scale less onerous in terms of capital expenses. New technologies and business practices now make it possible for capital-starved firms to go for larger production scales.

As more and more emerging market companies enter the global marketplace, we learn of new ways of leveraging scale, not just to cut costs but also to learn faster and design better products.

Betting on Scale in Consumer Electronics

Perhaps the most salient example of the power of scale is Samsung Electronics. Founded in 1969, this South Korean giant was a mere original equipment manufacturer for a variety of American brands—sold mostly at Sears, Wal-Mart, and Kmart—before it decided to take on Sony, Panasonic, Philips, and other well-established firms. Reaching global scale on the basis of an outsourcing business was essential to becoming large enough to invest in proprietary technology and brands.

Korean academic Sea-Jin Chang put it aptly: "Because the products it sells become commoditized so quickly, Samsung Electronics' strategic response to digital technology has been speed."[2] Samsung built up its manufacturing capabilities in memory chips during the 1990s, at a time when there was excess capacity worldwide. The company then moved quickly to capture market share from both existing and new customers. Samsung also integrated vertically, which lowered costs and helped the company bring products to market much faster. "We decided to focus all our resources in one product where we could do well," explained Yoon-Woo Lee, president of Samsung's semiconductor division. "We had to take a lot of risks. In addition, fortune was on our side. The timing was great."[3] (Notice the echoes of niche thinking here, the subject of our previous chapter.)

In 2001 revenue at Samsung Electronics reached $24.5 billion, still dwarfed by its European and Japanese competitors. By 2009 the company's revenues had soared to $110 billion, surpassing both Panasonic and Sony's. Philips meanwhile had been virtually forced to abandon many categories of components and mass-consumption electronic devices in favor of advanced lighting systems and medical devices. Most important, while its competitors were reporting large financial losses, Samsung's profits reached $7.6 billion. Over the past five years, no other company except IBM has been granted more patents.

Samsung Electronics is the poster child of the famous Miracle on the Han River, which catapulted South Korea from the Third World to the First within the scope of just one generation. It's also the brightest star in the Samsung *chaebol*, the Korean word for diversified business group. The word *samsung* itself means "three stars." Founded in 1938 as a trading company by Lee Byung-chull, the Samsung group now includes firms in every branch of the economy save for automobiles, which it tried to enter shortly before the Asian flu crisis of 1997.

Back in the late 1930s, however, Chairman Lee's firm was a grocery store that made its own noodles. At the time, Philips already was the global leader in lighting and other electrical goods. When Lee decided to invest in electronics in the 1960s, Panasonic was a global household brand. Talk about a long shot—but today Samsung Electronics is the global market leader in as many as 60 electronics product categories. The hallmark of its strategy has been to make large bets and move fast. No matter how daunting the challenge or how well prepared the competitors, Samsung has tended to win.

Examples of Samsung's audacity are so numerous that one wonders if it is even possible for one company to take so many areas by storm. In 2000 the firm started to make batteries for digital devices and became the global leader 10 years later. The company needed only four years to dominate the flat-panel TV set segment after entering in 2001. One year later Samsung invested in flash-memory chips, the technology that made the iPhone and the iPad possible, becoming Apple's largest supplier in fewer than five years. More recently, Samsung has surpassed fellow Korean firm LG as the world's number one maker of large-size LCD panels and of active-matrix organic light-emitting diode displays, used in mobile devices and TV sets, in which it has a whopping 97 percent global market share.

Samsung has created an entire mindset from fast entry into new areas with a view to building scale and moving on to the next exciting field. Unlike many of its competitors, this is not a company that breeds complacency. "The majority of our products today will be gone in 10 years," argued Lee Kun-hee, the second-generation chairman of the Samsung *chaebol*.[4] According to *The Economist*, the company is now intent on surging ahead of competitors in solar panels, automotive batteries, medical devices, and biotech. The up-front price tag for entering each of these fields can be as expensive as $7 billion.

Samsung Electronics has won big in high-growth, high-tech, and capital-intensive areas such as semiconductors and various types of displays. Like other emerging market companies, Samsung decided to build capacity fast by being a supplier to other firms as well as feeding components to its own divisions that make final consumer products.[5] "Samsung has realized economies of scale in both the memory chip and flat-screen sectors thanks to aggressive investments and faster decisions,"[6] said a top executive. The company is now in a position like no other firm to capitalize on economies of scope by making components closely related to those sectors, such as semiconductors and LCDs, whose manufacturing involves common activities such as deposition, photolithography, and etching integrated circuits. Moreover, these parts are used in a wide range of final products, including computers, digital cameras, and mobile phones, thus making it possible to reduce marketing expenses and enhance synergies in distribution logistics.

Samsung, however, is no longer content with being the world's favorite electronics component supplier. "TVs and mobile phones are the must-have items for general consumers," said a top executive. "The key points are how we will lead the markets and how to effectively read the minds of consumers. Coupled with our proven know-how in component-technologies and marketing and research capabilities, we will take a stronger stance toward the new shift."[7] Thus, Samsung is now trying to add such global electronics brands as Sony, Panasonic, and Nokia to its already long list of corporate victims, which includes Micron Technology, Advanced Micro Devices, Philips, Hitachi, Fujitsu, and Siemens. It has also chosen to compete in smart phones and tablet computers against Apple, one of its best clients.

Samsung Electronics epitomizes the modern, twenty-first-century company that leverages scale to become better at every stage of the value chain, from product design to manufacturing and logistics. You can certainly make mistakes when you build scale fast, especially about timing, and Samsung has made several along the way, including investments in certain plants before the market was ready or just after a downturn began. This, of course, is the nature of the beast with large investments in electronics, a product category very prone to cyclicality. Unlike other companies, though, Samsung has been nimble about exiting from its errors, and it has made far fewer of them than competitors such as Sony, Nokia, HP, and Dell. Plus, when you grow by placing dozens of high-stake bets on specific, yet interrelated, product categories, you stand a better chance of crowning your efforts with success. Product scope helps manage the potential pitfalls of scale.

Samsung's obsession with scale is in part attributable to the peculiarities of the Korean business landscape. Starting during the Japanese occupation, the Korean *chaebol* made a habit of emulating and imitating one another. This pattern became more pronounced under General Park Chung-hee, who ruled South Korea between 1963 and 1979, the period of most intense industrialization. The various *chaebol*—Hyundai, Samsung, LG,

Daewoo, Sunkyong—followed each other to new industries, beginning with clothing and footwear; then simple assembled goods and electronics; later, heavy industry, construction, and shipbuilding; and finally automobiles. This process was to a large extent orchestrated by the government, which offered subsidized loans at *negative* real interest rates as low as minus 15 percent, meaning that after taking inflation into account the borrowers only returned 85 percent of the principal.

"We always try to get free money," the president of Daewoo told us back in 1997, a few months before the infamous Asian flu crisis.[8] It goes without saying that if someone gives you free money, you may as well take as much of it as possible to set up the most capital-intensive factories you can imagine. Although the subsidized-loan programs were phased out in the early 1990s, the habit and mindset of investing in large industrial under-takings endured. Samsung Electronics is clearly a child of this South Korean setting, yet to its credit, it grew up very quickly to become a major global corporation.[9] By contrast, many com-panies affiliated with the Hyundai and Daewoo *chaebol* perished in the 1997 crisis.

Scaling to Win in Traditional Industries

Building scale fast can work wonders in traditional industries too, not just in those churning out high-tech gadgetry. Consider the example of Arcor, the world's largest candy manufacturing company. Fulvio Pagani started the firm in 1951 in a sleepy, tiny town in the pampa flatlands of Argentina—that is, pretty much in the middle of nowhere. Pagani's father, who had emigrated from Italy, set up a small bakery in the 1920s, where his five children worked after reaching age 10. Several family members decided that the future lay in building a large factory in order to reduce costs. The Arcor name was formed by combining the first letters of the town, Arroyito, with those of the province in which it is situated, Córdoba.

Founded as it was in the Argentina of the time, the odds were stacked against Arcor. Labor costs were high because of President Juan Domingo Perón's labor laws,[10] procuring machinery from abroad was prohibitively expensive, and securing the necessary raw materials and inputs was a nightmare in a country with few reliable suppliers and poor infrastructure—the company even had to build its own gas pipeline!

Schooled in the hard realities of one of the most volatile emerging economies over a period of two decades, the company started to export in the 1960s and to invest in foreign distribution and production in the mid-1970s. One of the company's slogans is "From a candy, Arcor made a world." And so it has been. Arcor now operates 40 plants in Argentina, Brazil, Chile, Peru, and Mexico, and it is causing cavities in 120 export markets, with its extensive range of hard and soft candies, caramels, pralines, nougats, biscuits and cookies, molded chocolates and tablets, jellies, and gums. The company also makes private-label candies for Wal-Mart, Sara Lee, and Brach's Confections, among others. In 2000, Luis Pagani was inducted into the Candy Hall of Fame, the highest honor conferred by the National Confectionery Sales Association in the United States.

As with so many other emerging market multinationals, Arcor's success has much to do with turning weaknesses into strengths. Mired by high labor costs and unreliable suppliers, the company concentrated its efforts on a few products and built scale fast so as to justify the costs of vertical integration into everything from wheat, flour, sugar, eggs, and dairy to cardboards for packaging. Although it was initially not efficient, operating along the value chain enabled Arcor managers to fully understand the bottlenecks and the critical path links. "Vertical integration is a means to greater stability in the supplying of raw materials and packing," explained CEO Pagani.

"It is a way to diminish the level of uncertainty in the supply chain."[11] For a firm making three million pounds of products *daily* (up from 120,000 during its first decade) as well as a half-million pounds of paper and cardboard to feed its wrapping and packaging lines, controlling and understanding the linkages along the value chain is a key source of competitive advantage.

Scale and vertical integration have also allowed Arcor to exploit its own excess production capacity. "Our vertical integration strategy helped us gain additional sources of income once the production levels surpassed the Group's own consumption needs,"[12] observed Pagani. This is a principle that Swatch, the famed Swiss watch manufacturer and brand, also found useful for optimizing its manufacturing operations. Swatch sells as many as 100 million watch movements each year to lower-cost producers around the world.

Vertical integration has yet another advantage, Pagani said: "We ensure transparency with regards to prices, and we get to know the degree of competitiveness of our businesses. As a rule, every Arcor business has to have market prices."[13]

Companies that outsource production to Arcor go out of their way to praise the Argentine company. "We looked at firms in Mexico and elsewhere offering greater savings," said Kevin Kotecki, president of Brach's Confections, "but Arcor's reputation for quality and reliability mattered more."[14] The two firms started their collaboration in 2001 after Brach's shut down its Chicago candy plant.

While machinery and automation enabled the company to reduce costs so as to be competitive in Argentina and neighboring Latin American markets, such heavy capital investment also required large production runs, high-capacity utilization, and inordinate attention to every detail of the manufacturing operations: mixing, heating, evaporating, shaping, cooling, wrapping, and boxing candy for children of all ages around the world. "Even

Nestlé and Kraft admit we are efficient," boasted Pagani.[15] "Arcor concentrated on industrial know-how, productivity, and cost reduction—its key DNA components."[16] Today, its candy factory in Arroyito is the largest in the world. According to *Business Week*, "The sprawling, 78,000-square-meter facility is a model of efficiency." Kotecki of Brach's concurred: "Quite frankly, they have the capacity and technology to do things we can't."[17]

Manufacturing prowess, however, was not enough to crack markets around the world. Quality improvements and product differentiation through branding were needed for entry into the more sophisticated markets of North America and Europe. "In the 1993–2000 period, we entered into a more marketing-oriented stage, seeking to position Arcor's brand name and introduce changes into our marketing strategies," said Pagani. "Marketing was our weakness, and new players in the industry were forcing us to step up our marketing practices."[18] They determined that the big global firms in the industry lacked the scale to be the leaders in candy. "When we saw an opening, we were prepared to compete head to head with the multinationals."[19]

That's a story repeated time and again by the emerging market multinationals we studied. These are companies that saw an opening and took it, without over-worrying about the risks. Like other companies that excelled at execution in order to become global champions—Bimbo, Embraer, and Samsung prominent among them—"Arcor learned how to sell to foreign markets, adapting itself to different habits and cultures by trial and error," in Luis Pagani's words. "The world is our market," he likes to assert, but that "world market" is really made up of a multitude of very discrete markets.[20]

Indeed, one of Arcor's key strengths has been its ability to tailor products to the specific characteristics of the 120 markets the company serves. Executives choose a different branding and distribution strategy for each market. In some they collaborate with local firms in manufacturing and distribution, as in

Mexico, where they run a plant jointly with Bimbo.[21] By contrast, Kraft-Cadbury stumbled in Latin America during the 1990s and the first decade of the new millennium by going it alone and trying to impose on consumers global candy brands. Executives there were too proud of their global brand strategy to admit it was not working, even as the evidence piled up that markets were fragmented and different from those they were used to. When it comes to candy, you need to be efficient and attentive to local tastes.

Arcor's main challenge, however, is to ride the wave of growth in the emerging economies of Asia as its consumer markets develop. While the company exports candy to those markets, its presence pales by comparison to Arcor's strong showing in its home region of Latin America.

The Answer is Blowin' in the Wind . . .

Being an innovator is all about seizing the spirit of the time. Bob Dylan did just that by capturing in his lyrics the mixed mystical and rebellious nature of the 1960s and early 1970s. So did India's Suzlon during the first decade of the twenty-first century, the latest and fastest-growing wind turbine manufacturer, a company that has seized the spirit of clean, renewable energy to grow and prosper.

Contrary to appearances, generating electricity from wind is an exceedingly complex activity involving turbine manufacturers, wind-farm developers, constructors and operators, power distributors, and government regulators. The viability of wind power depends on multiple critical factors, ranging from technology to demand conditions, and from regulation to the structure of competition. In addition, the wind industry would never have been developed without the support of national governments via tax incentives and subsidies.

Companies from emerging economies have revolutionized competitive dynamics in this high-tech, high-growth industry. Consider the example of GE Wind, the world's third-largest firm. Seeing its competitive edge erode over time, the whole of GE recently started a program aimed at generating innovations from emerging countries. "If GE doesn't come up with innovations in poor countries and take them global," noted Jeffrey R. Immelt, chairman and CEO, "new competitors from the developing world—like Mindray, Suzlon, Goldwind, and Haier—will." Reflecting on the dangers associated with growing competition from emerging countries, he added that "GE has tremendous respect for traditional rivals like Siemens, Philips, and Rolls-Royce. But it knows how to compete with them; they will never destroy GE. By introducing products that create a new price-performance paradigm, however, the emerging giants very well could."[22]

Wise words. Emerging market companies in the wind industry are gaining ground thanks to innovative strategies related to technology development and the supply chain. Wind turbine manufacturers differ from one another in terms of their degree of vertical integration—backward into component manufacturing (rotor blades, gearboxes, generators, control systems, and a number of other components) and/or forward into wind-farm development and operation. They're also different in terms of whether they possess their own technology or not.

"In 2003, we altered the business slightly to extend our service all the way through the supply chain," explained Suzlon's CEO, Tulsi R. Tanti. "We decided to make the components of wind turbines, too, to get vertical integration that would ramp up supply very fast."[23] Being passionate, even irrationally so, about this ancient, yet largely untapped, source of energy was integral to Suzlon's success.

The origins of Suzlon are somewhat atypical. In 1995 Tanti decided to set aside his traditional textile business (which would be sold in 2001) to start a company providing end-to-end services in the development of wind farms. It was not the leap into the unknown that it appeared to be. Tired of the inefficient, erratic, and expensive power supply of India's state-owned electricity network, Tanti had built a wind-power infrastructure to satisfy the demand of his own textile business. He realized that his expertise in doing so would benefit any company in the world willing to invest in wind farms. While he lacked any technological background in the industry, his main advantage was that he had experience when it came to managing the whole process of building the installation from the beginning to the end. His expertise was unique because none of the existing wind-power firms were vertically integrated—they just supplied the turbine, made the installation, or performed maintenance. That's how Suzlon became an end-to-end turnkey contractor, taking care of every task, from supplying the equipment to finding the right location for the wind farm and building, operating, and maintaining the facilities.

Once put into practice, this strategy of vertical integration led the company to produce the entire set of components in the wind turbines. Making every gadget along the value chain further enabled Suzlon to control costs and avoid bottlenecks in a market that grows at the speed of light—nearly 30 percent a year.

"The normal business model in this industry is turbine technology and assembly," said Tanti. "They then outsource the components required for the wind turbines. They don't have access to the component technology. The real technology part is in the components. So if you own the two technologies, and integrate the two, then you have the most competitive product, which is reliable and next generation. . . . To grow the supply chain is the key bottleneck in the industry."[24]

But vertical integration across so many manufacturing and service activities is not possible without a solid proprietary technological base. And one cannot justify the immense cost of developing technology without attaining a large scale of operation. Suzlon is expanding both in India, the world's third-fastest growing market, and internationally in order to meet this challenge. In fact, the expansion has been explosive: the Indian company is now the sixth fastest growing in the world. Suzlon already is number one in India, number two in the United Kingdom, and number three in France and in Germany in terms of new installations. The company has entered into a virtuous cycle in which global scale and vertical integration mutually reinforce each other and play in favor of the company.

"The skeleton of our cost structure is built on low cost. . . . I run with 65 percent material costs. The industry benchmark is 70–80 percent. That makes me 5 percent more efficient. Power cost globally is 8–9 percent. My cost is not more than 4 percent. That makes me at least 10 percent more competitive than anybody else in the world,"[25] said Tanti.

Suzlon has been anything but shy when it comes to ensuring that it has the necessary technology available to support its strategy of vertical integration and global growth. First, it licensed technology. Then it looked for acquisition targets. More recently, it has built its own R&D capabilities. The company started producing its own wind turbines under license from Germany's Subwind in 1995 and also obtained licenses for manufacturing rotor blades.

Critical to its success, Suzlon was not a passive licensee. The company tried to fully assimilate the external knowledge and started to build R&D centers not only in India but also in Europe, to be close to new technological developments. Suzlon located in Germany for wind turbines and in the Netherlands for rotor blades. In 2006 the company acquired Hansen Transmissions, a Danish gearbox manufacturer, establishing at the same time an R&D center there. And finally in 2008 it acquired REpower, a German company focused on manufacturing offshore and high-capacity wind turbines. Suzlon also located its international headquarters in Denmark. These investments in Europe made the company more visible, but above all, they made it easier to be in touch with the latest developments in the industry.

In addition to taking over REpower, the international expansion of Suzlon has been based on the establishment of subsidiaries in the most important markets, including the United States, Brazil, Spain, Portugal, Italy, Denmark, and China, where the government requires local production in order to access the market. While all this happened, Suzlon kept the bulk of its manufacturing activities in India, turning itself into the only dual-shore company in the industry.

Suzlon's swift rise to global prominence in the wind-power industry stands in stark contrast with the long and winding road taken by Western European and American firms. The world's leading turbine manufacturer is Vestas Wind Systems A/S, a Danish firm engaged in design and manufacturing, but not in wind-farm development and operation. The fact that Vestas is based in Denmark—a country, along with the State of California, at the forefront in the development of wind power— gives the company a big leg up in the industry. But while Vestas grew to become the world's number one firm over a period of more than 30 years, Suzlon has needed only a little more than a decade to catapult itself to the top ranks of the industry. Thanks to its aggressive policy of external growth, Suzlon is nowadays able to manufacture the same range of components and products as Vestas despite the Danish firm's huge initial technological disadvantage. (Suzlon's decision to relocate its headquarters to Denmark could be seen as serving notice that the competition with Vestas has just begun.) Suzlon is also catching up fast with GE Wind, the only American firm among the world's top 10.

This aggressive growth strategy was funded through an equally aggressive debt strategy, but the company didn't throw caution to the wind altogether. Suzlon's purchase of REpower was typical of its approach. Initially, Suzlon acquired one-third of the German company's equity along with the option of acquiring the remaining two-thirds within two years.

Suzlon's fast growth has also exposed it to some unforeseen pitfalls. Acquiring REpower through the backdoor left Suzlon sometimes battling with other minority shareholders over strategy and targets. In addition, the global financial crisis has slowed down wind-farm development in Europe, forcing the heavily indebted Suzlon to focus more on emerging markets. Other problems have to do with top management turnover and the reliability of Suzlon's rotor blades. Some blades manufactured by Suzlon and installed in United States wind parks cracked under extreme cold weather conditions. Other companies in the industry have faced similar problems with their blades in these locations—and of course, a cracked wind-turbine blade is far less of a danger than a cracked airplane propeller blade—but the mishap still took a toll on Suzlon's order book and reputation after it was made public in 2008.

To deal with these problems the company has reorganized itself in a number of ways. "If I am in a growth situation, then I cannot consolidate my organization, and for the past decade we had just been growing," Tanti said. "So, now I have the chance to build the organization for the next 10 years—because a lot of change is needed, like product, organizational structure, management bandwidth, and resource planning."[26] Suzlon decided to compensate for its lack of resources by selling Hansen Transmission and taking full control of REpower so it could fully implement a program to prevent further problems with the rotor blades.

"REpower is just a turbine manufacturer. Suzlon has competencies in component technologies and manufacturing of towers, rotor blades, control panels . . . So we can integrate seamlessly," said Tanti. "The key is to integrate these strengths as it gives the market a reliable and cost-competitive product."[27] On the contrary, Suzlon never tried to integrate Hansen within its structure. "Hansen Transmissions is in a different business . . . Hansen being an independent company gives huge comfort to other customers, including leading wind-turbine makers like Vestas and Gamesa,"[28] said Tanti in 2008. The divestment in Hansen was progressive. First the company launched an IPO in the London Stock Exchange in 2007, and minority stakes were sold progressively until 2011. It made sense. Gearboxes are critical components for wind turbines, but Suzlon could not fully capture the value of REpower without being the sole owner. For this reason, it turned a control relationship into a strategic alliance by keeping a long-term supply agreement with Hansen.

The main challenges nowadays lie in emerging markets, especially China. The race for global leadership is on because Chinese firms Sinovel and Goldwind have become larger than Suzlon thanks to growth in the domestic market, the world's largest and fastest growing—doubling in size each year for the past three years. Suzlon has recently appointed a local manager, He Yaozu, as its CEO in China. "Suzlon's operations in China feature a good combination of strengths from both developed and developing worlds," said He. "Compared with international players, Suzlon comes from the developing world and is therefore more familiar with China's general market and more adaptable to its local market. Compared with local players, our products are embedded with cutting-edge wind technology."[29] Suzlon is so far the only emerging market competitor with this combination of assets and capabilities, though it won't take long for its Chinese competitors, especially Sinovel and Windstar, to catch up.

Suzlon's meteoric rise illustrates the power of combining vertical integration, global scale, and sustained growth. Vertical integration and global scale were not means by themselves but means to an end: growth and competitiveness. For Suzlon, vertical integration and global scope reinforced the firm's growth prospects because they helped keep costs under control and reduce bottlenecks. But the main advantage of global scale for the company has been the possibility of changing the rules of the game in the industry once it managed to (a) absorb the state-of-the-art technological knowledge offered by developed countries and (b) then combine that knowledge with the stunning manufacturing capabilities and advantages inherent to emerging economies. And there's more. Scale and vertical integration have also given Suzlon an important competitive advantage against newcomers seeking to compete in the same market. As one consultant to the India's wind-energy industry observed, "A new player coming in will have a huge entry barrier due to complete end-to-end solutions provided by players such as Suzlon." Entering a new country, in his view, "is not an issue of supply and demand."[30]

Winning by Growing Big, Fast

While scale is no panacea, most people underestimate its benefits. We've learned from Samsung, Arcor, and Suzlon that it's not just about lowering unit costs; it's really about building a strong foundation for continued growth, as shown in Figure 3.

- Increased scale can have almost magical effects on both costs and competitive capabilities. High volumes enable the firm to move faster down the learning curve than competitors, even when everyone is learning the same thing. Arcor, for example, learned faster because it was bigger, *and* it made sure that all of its plants throughout Latin America shared knowledge and experience.
- Most important, scale preempts competitors from invading your space. Samsung benefited from this effect by convincing potential competitors that the semiconductor industry was becoming too crowded. Scale thus helps build entry barriers to newcomers, and when combined

FIGURE 3

Building up the pyramid of scale.

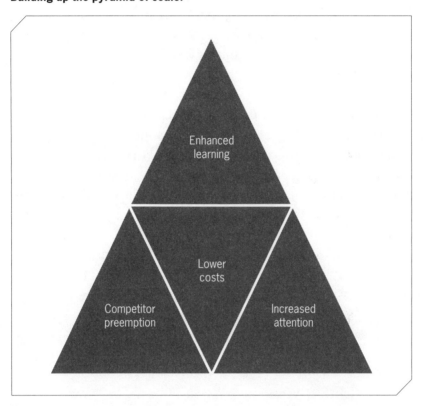

with vertical integration, as the Suzlon case shows, the barriers become even steeper.

- Perhaps the most neglected potential benefit of scale is that it brings attention to your company and its products, signaling to suppliers and customers alike that you must be taken seriously. Scale gives you stature and presence. Suzlon was taken seriously by customers, suppliers, and competitors alike only after it signaled its seriousness by ramping up scale. You may even gain in bargaining power as you grow bigger, assuming you do not have to rely on just one supplier or one customer. What's more, reaching global scale across developed and emerging markets quickly may allow your company to be the first at combining and exploiting the best of both worlds—that is, state-of-the-art technology and low-cost manufacturing skills.

And don't forget the most important point of all: scale today is always defined on a global basis. Thus, in order to gain global scale quickly, you must enter international markets from day one. Companies such as Samsung, Arcor, Suzlon, and Infosys, among many others highlighted in this book, developed business plans aimed at competing against global leaders for a share of the world market. If you want to be a winner, you must develop your value proposition relative to that of global leaders.

Embrace Chaos

Learn and profit from adverse institutional environments.

If you have something at risk, you think differently.

—HENRY KRAVIS

Chaos is a friend of mine.

—BOB DYLAN

O NCE UPON A TIME, WAY BACK IN THE TWENTIETH CEN-
tury, there were safe markets and there were risky ones.
Safe markets offered predictability, minimal government inter-
ference, and a good infrastructure for doing business. Risky
markets were mostly in the developing world, where governments often made capricious decisions, placed myriad obstacles
for entrepreneurs, and lacked the minimal legal, financial, transportation, and telecommunications infrastructure for firms to
operate.

Welcome to the twenty-first century. In multiple arenas of
the global economy, the line separating safe and risky markets
has become blurred, almost to the point of extinction. Many
developed countries—the United States included—have chaotic and unpredictable governments, some so deeply in debt

89

that they have let critical infrastructure become dilapidated over time. Stock markets, too, are no longer easily characterized as either safe or risky. More and more, financial-market volatility is global, not local.

While developed economies are sinking toward a world mean, many emerging economies have been rising to meet them and in some cases surpass them. Numerous developing nations have built a world-class infrastructure in areas such as ports, telecommunications, airports, high-speed rail, and business parks. In many of them, governments are not as unpredictable as they once were. Companies that learned the ropes in developing and emerging markets are capitalizing on these confusing trends. They've learned to live with chaos.

As we've already seen, Argentina's Arcor, the world's largest candy manufacturer, had no choice but to set up its supply chain from scratch. Its home country is notoriously unpredictable: more than 25 different presidents and 50 economy ministers have held office since World War II. Economic and trade policies abruptly changed every three or four years. Hyperinflation reached nearly 4,000 percent in 1989. "One of the main conditions for managing firms in Argentina is to be flexible, that is, to know how to adapt quickly to changes," observed Luis Pagani, Arcor's second-generation CEO. "With high inflation rates, the capacity to be flexible and to react quickly to changes is very important."[1] Other companies we looked at in previous chapters—Bimbo, Suzlon, and Haier—were similarly toughened by the vicissitudes of conducting business in at least semihostile, frequently chaotic environments.

Street smarts, of course, are not the exclusive property of emerging markets. Spain's Telefónica, the world's third-largest telecommunications operator, grew internationally by focusing on Latin America, a region widely perceived to be too risky at the time. In 1995, while the executives of North American firms were being driven around Peru's capital in armored cars,

Telefónica's top brass walked around town unhurriedly and eventually made a bid for the state-owned telephone company more than twice as high as that by GTE and Southwestern Bell. "Telefónica had a very different idea of risk," both in financial and in personal terms, Iñaki Santillana, former CEO for international expansion, told us.[2]

No one would accuse Ikea, the world's largest furnishings retailer, of having developing market roots, either. Sweden is first world all the way. But when the company's home-country suppliers imposed a boycott because of the firm's harsh negotiation tactics, Ikea responded by adopting an emerging market mindset. Instead of fretting over the boycott, Ikea opted to pursue foreign sourcing and market opportunities, and let the disgruntled suppliers stew in their own juices. "Who knows what problems can do for you?" assert the authors of *The Viking Manifesto*, a study of Swedish management practices.

But while multinationals like Telefónica and Ikea show that the old guard can embrace and profit from chaotic environments, emerging market multinationals have perfected the art of doing so. Let us learn from Acer's meteoric rise to the number two spot in worldwide personal computer sales, Orascom Telecom's daring investments in Iraq and North Korea, and Bharat Forge's vicissitudes in some of the world's most difficult markets.

A Dragon Takes Over the Personal Computer Industry

The story of Acer is one of the most tantalizing among emerging market multinationals. The firm was founded in the 1970s when Taiwan was a developing country struggling to find a place for itself in the global economy. Back in 1999, the company had a mere 3 percent global market share, the tenth largest. Nowadays, it commands a 13 percent share, second only to Hewlett-Packard's

19 percent and closely followed by Dell with 12 percent and Lenovo of China with 10 percent.

In spite of being only 30 years old, the personal computer industry is very mature and commoditized. To succeed, you need to take risks, be bold, and engage the customer. As a contributor to the Chief Officers' Network once put it, "The computer industry is like the fashion industry: It's driven not by needs but by wants."[3] Like clothing companies, computer makers use planned obsolescence as a competitive weapon. You can't run the latest software on an old computer, so you are compelled to upgrade your hardware. As with fashion, novelty and style are also vital to computer sales.

How, then, did Acer break into the top rank of this fashion-driven industry in spite of the technological and funding constraints it faced throughout its formative years? Instead of asking for loans, it maxed out retained earnings and invested abroad in collaboration with equity joint-venture partners. In the end, scarce capital proved to be a blessing in disguise. Yes, it carried risk, but the absence of ready funding taught the company how to economize on almost everything while developing new ways of expanding abroad. Acer learned to do more with less.

"Global expansion entails facing various challenges and requires making choices all the time," explained Stan Shih, founder of Acer. "For a company pursuing sustainable growth, all kinds of risks will follow, like a shadow. But if you don't take risks, what you create can be quite limited."[4] *Fortune* magazine once described Shih as "a fascinating combination of engineering nerd, traditional Chinese businessman, avant-garde manager, and international entrepreneur, with an outsize ambition and vision to match."[5] He and his company are also very much made in Taiwan.

Taiwanese electronics firms, of which Acer is the largest and most successful, make two-thirds of the world's notebook PCs and cable modems, and one-third of all digital cameras and servers. They also manufacture the overwhelming majority of computer components, such as motherboards and LCD monitors. Like other Taiwanese firms, Acer used to make all of its products in Taiwan but has more recently shifted production to China and Southeast Asia.

Acer was founded in 1976 as Multitech, a distributor of electronic parts. Five years later, Shih changed the company's name to Acer, from the Latin for "sharp," and in 1983, Shih launched an IBM clone. At the time the company relied on outsourcing to IBM, Dell, Fujitsu, Hitachi, and Siemens for most of its revenue. All that began to change in 1987, when the company began marketing its first Acer-branded computer. In 1993, the company entered into a joint venture with Texas Instruments to manufacture DRAMs, setting up Taiwan's first dynamic random access memory-chip fabrication plant, or "fab." For several years, chips delivered windfall profits, but this investment turned into a liability when a glut developed in the global market after 1995.

Shih realized that high transportation costs; falling prices for processors, hard drives, and motherboards; high inventory expenses; and low margins required a new strategy. Under his Fresh Technology for Everyone campaign, Acer would put together the PC at local assembly facilities, using the most up-to-date components only after a customer had placed an order. In fact, Acer used to put an employee on a flight from Miami to each of its Latin American assembly facilities, carrying up to 1,000 Intel chips needed to meet customer demand on a just-in-time basis. Only nonperishable parts such as keyboards, mice, casings, and power supplies would be stocked on location. This fast-food approach earned Shih the title "the Ray Kroc of the PC business." By emulating McDonald's, the company reduced cycle times so that it could boot the computer just two hours after it was ordered.

Foreign expansion with decentralized and locally owned subsidiaries had made Acer scattered and complex. Seeing administrative costs skyrocket, Shih retired and brought in

Leonard Liu as president of Acer Group and CEO of its U.S. subsidiary. A Princeton-trained PhD in computer science, Liu had been the highest-ranking Chinese-American at IBM. Rather than embracing Shih's managerial philosophy of extensive delegation without accountability, and his emphasis on harmony, trust, loyalty, and employee-stock ownership, Liu insisted on establishing a panoply of organizational and financial controls, with the ultimate goal of turning Acer into a little Big Blue. Acer, however, didn't need more bureaucracy. It needed a new strategy to succeed in a fiercely competitive global market with falling margins. Managers in Taiwan rebelled, dubbing Liu and his lieutenants the "parachute managers." Liu lasted three years on the job, forcing Shih to stage a comeback. "In 1989, I thought IBM was the best-managed company in our field," recalled Shih. "I supposed that Liu was more experienced and capable than I, but he was not an entrepreneur."[6]

Shih decided to encourage his managers to design and launch new, innovative products. The Aspire computer, launched in 1995, was the biggest bet: a PC ahead of its time, designed as a home computer, Internet-enabled, and loaded with multimedia and voice-recognition applications. Runaway costs and lack of marketing savvy made it difficult for Acer to make money with the Aspire. The iMac, launched in 1998, stole the show, captivating a similar market of users eager for an easy-to-use home computer. Moreover, the iMac was cute, while Aspire was an ugly duckling. Acer lost over $100 million with the Aspire before pulling it out of the U.S. market in early 1999. Yet another problem with Acer's strategy had to do with its dual role as a supplier for and competitor with IBM, Dell, and HP. The Acer brand was competing for customers against the very PCs that it made in Taiwan for the American brands.

In fact, Acer was still swimming upstream, struggling to emerge from its birth in a developing market, but what held the company back was also Acer's latent strength. Operating in chaotic environments characterized by inflation, changing regulations, and sharp macroeconomic shocks had taught the company to be nimble and to evolve as circumstances required, and in 2001 Shih began to put that experience into play.

He started by spinning off all manufacturing activities while keeping design and selling of Acer-branded computers within the Acer company itself. He created Wistron Corp.—a name concocted from the combination of *wisdom* and *electronics*—which focused on contract manufacturing of PCs, servers, PDAs, set-top boxes, and circuit boards. He also founded BenQ—*bringing enjoyment* and *quality*—to take over the manufacturing of mobile phones, displays, notebook computers, flash drives, and scanners. Both spin-offs were eventually listed on the stock market, with Acer reducing its equity interest to a nominal stake.

The reorganization paid off handsomely. Acer could now pursue its dreams of becoming a truly global brand by focusing on design and selling. Its personal computers would be manufactured by Wistron or BenQ, which would also continue to serve the needs of IBM, Dell, and HP. In 2005, Shih installed a fresh management team, including J. T. Wang as chairman and Gianfranco Lanci as CEO. Armed with its new strategy of totally separating design and selling from manufacturing, and the additional capital raised through the spin-offs, Acer could now go on a shopping spree. In 2007 it acquired Gateway for $710 million, a key addition to Acer's already strong positions in Europe and Asia. The acquisition enabled Acer to have an "effective multibrand strategy and cover all the major market segments," in the words of Lanci.[7] Then Acer acquired Packard Bell, E-TEN, and nearly 30 percent of Olidata. In October 2009, Acer surpassed Dell to become the world's second-ranked PC brand, a major accomplishment for an emerging market multinational.

Acer's distinctive approach to decision making enabled it to cope with the chaos of operating across so many emerging economies with different local partners in each of them. "Conflict and disagreement will inevitably occur during the transformation of a company," Shih wrote in his book, *Me-Too Is Not My Style.* "If executives treat conflict from a pessimistic viewpoint, they would rather settle disputes in fear that chaos may occur. To view it from the optimistic side, conflict is the process of building consensus."[8]

Chaos was also something Acer had to contend with at home. The mercurial political situation in Taiwan and the uncertainty surrounding the future status of the island weighed heavily in the firm's decision in the mid-1990s to locate manufacturing abroad, as a hedge against tensions with China over Taiwan's first presidential election in 1996. In a U.S. diplomatic cable dated August 2006, and made public by WikiLeaks, Shih "described the current political situation in Taiwan as chaotic," adding that "he didn't have time to complain." Instead, the cable reads, "He views political uncertainty as one of the limitations of the business environment he has to operate in." But those same limitations were also constantly schooling Shih and Acer for life on a far bigger stage.

Acer took significant risks in over 20 Latin American and Southeast Asian emerging economies, honing skills in the developing world before entering the hyperdeveloped U.S. market. "We decentralized our management to local branches and gave them discretionary authorization to make independent decisions. We also decentralized our purchasing, assembly, and production activities. We abandoned the strategy of sole-venture channel expansion and allowed joint-venture partners to hold greater shares in our subsidiaries and to join our strategy-making and execution," explained Shih, looking back at two decades of rapid and chaotic growth. "Although we made a big detour before entering the U.S. market, we built a solid foundation in peripheral areas and accumulated tremendous internationalization strength, which in turn helped us finally secure an advantageous position in the global market."[9]

The Egyptian Challenger in Telecommunications

In regulated industries such as telecommunications, emerging market companies such as Egypt's Orascom Telecommunications Holding (OTH), Mexico's América Móvil, and India's Tata Communications abound. These companies have excelled at expanding into other emerging economies, while giants such as Vodafone and AT&T have shied away from many of these risky markets. Why? Because even though established multinationals may have deeper experience when it comes to operating telecommunications networks, they find it difficult to expand into countries with weak institutional environments in which politicians and regulators have high levels of discretion and important gaps exist in the development of the infrastructure. Their comfort level is found in completely different environments: countries with basic infrastructures already developed and stable regulatory conditions, so that initial investment is low and changes in the rules of the game are less likely.

Years ago, for instance, U.S. telecommunications giant AT&T sold its Latin American assets to the Mexican group that owns América Móvil. The U.S. firm retained a minority stake in América Móvil and kept some collaborative links with the Mexican upstart, but this move was basically a concession that AT&T simply wasn't as adept as América Móvil at turning a profit in an unpredictable environment. In 2010, Randall Stephenson, chairman and CEO of AT&T, crowed that "We have a major stake in Latin America through América Móvil, and it contributes a lot to our earnings and our cash flow,"[10] but really he was just making the best of the same bad situation encountered by other old-line telecommunications firms seeking to operate in Latin-American and other emerging markets.

Consider the case of Orascom Telecom Holding, the Egyptian giant. It is hard to explain the growth of this company without taking into account its ability to operate in weak institutional environments subject to unusually high levels of risk such as Iraq and North Korea.

The origins of Orascom lie in a Cairo-based construction firm established in 1950 by Onsi Sawiris. While developing and building everything from dams and highways to shopping malls, the company acquired two capabilities that are invaluable to the telecommunications industry: experience in the execution of infrastructure projects and experience in dealing with politicians and regulators. Sawiris got a taste of political risk in 1971 when his business was nationalized. Five years later, under a new political regime more favorable to private business, he formed a second construction company that became the starting point of Orascom Group, a diversified conglomerate with three arms: Orascom Telecom Holding, Orascom Construction Industries, and Orascom Hotels and Development, each run by one of his sons. In the process, Sawiris became a legend in Egyptian business circles: "He's a fighter; he started three times in his life," his oldest son, Naguib, told interviewer Charlie Rose.[11]

Even though the Orascom Group had a presence in the IT field trading and distributing IT and telecommunications equipment, the company became a telecommunications service provider through acquisitions, not by growing from within. Its first foray was the purchase of InTouch, a domestic Internet service provider. In 1998, teamed up with Motorola and France Télécom, Orascom won the bid for the privatization of 51 percent of ECMS (Egyptian Company for Mobile Services), also known as Mobinil. So far, the story of Orascom might sound like the standard business saga of a well-connected family in a developing economy, but there's much more to it than garden-variety cronyism.

In 1998, Onsi Sawiris stepped down after installing Naguib as chairman and CEO of Orascom Telecom Holding. Naguib was the one who realized the huge potential of telecommunications in emerging markets, thanks to the confluence of two factors. First, the lack of a preexisting telecommunications infrastructure and the flexibility of mobile networks meant faster growth than in the developed world. "Fixed lines were never available in our part of the world," he said. "When the mobiles came, they overgrew the fixed line . . . so now the use is mostly on the cellular and not on the fixed line."[12] The second factor, he continued, was that established firms were reluctant to enter these countries because of the risks and also because, if they dared enter, they would not be patient enough to harvest the fruits. In his view, many companies that "ventured in Latin America sold too early. They didn't understand the value of being in highly populated countries. . . . For me, [it] was a simple calculation. I knew [what's] going to happen in our part of the world—we have more population, and revenues are going to be higher, and growth is going to be higher."

Obviously, the risks were higher too, along with the returns, but the takeaway point is that Orascom was willing to go down this path only because of its experience in Egypt. "If you come from a risky destination, then the risk is relative," Naguib Sawiris explained. "I remember when I went to Algeria, and they told me they were killing people there, and there are some bombs, and I said, 'This is everyday news in my part of the world, so what's the big deal?'"

From its highly educational home platform, Orascom started to expand into other emerging and risky countries that shared two features: high-growth potential and little competition. Sometimes these features were accompanied by weak institutional environments, which meant that once the investment was made, the rules of the game could change at any time. But Orascom and other companies in the telecommunications industry discovered that governments were in fact interested in developing infrastructure and would handsomely reward companies that helped them do so.

Over the first decade of the new century, Orascom Telecom entered countries that are a roster of global hotspots: Jordan,

Yemen, Pakistan, Zimbawe (with the acquisition of Telecel, which included 11 licenses to operate in several sub-Saharan African countries), Algeria, Tunisia, Iraq, Bangladesh, North Korea, Burundi, the Central African Republic, Namibia, and Lebanon. One would be hard-pressed to find another company in any industry that exposed itself to such epic risks in so many chaotic countries. The Sawiris family also invested in Italy's Wind Telecomunicazioni S.p.A. (which also operates in Greece and Belgium) in 2005 and, in 2010, merged Wind and Orascom with Russian operator Vimpelcom, becoming the sixth-largest mobile operator in the world.

There's no mystery why established firms chose not to enter the countries in which Orascom has flourished: they would be at a distinct disadvantage if they did. Orascom's entry into North Korea is illustrative: the company's Egyptian roots gave it a large edge over Vodafone and other competitors, and its willingness to develop a telecommunications infrastructure where virtually none existed won expressions of gratitude from the Dear Leader. No country is more closed to foreign investment and capitalism than North Korea, yet Orascom managed to develop a positive relationship with the government. How?

The good vibes began when Orascom Construction Industries was developing projects in China close to the North Korean border. The company established negotiations with the North Korean government and in 2007 agreed to invest $115 million in a cement plant in exchange for 50 percent of its equity. The money was directed to modernize the facilities. As part of the deal, Orascom Construction was allowed to use North Korean labor in its China projects. The arrangement allowed Orascom to get to learn about the government's plans to promote infrastructure projects as well as to establish trust with politicians and regulators. Orascom was eventually granted a 25-year license with an exclusivity period of four years, without any licensing fee, although with the commitment to develop the telecommunications network.

"With no competition and no licensing fees, it was a golden opportunity for OTH," said Hassan Abdou, CEO of Orascom's parent holding company, Weather Investments II. The North Korean project, he added, "is, in fact, relatively low-risk when compared to the potential reward. In most other countries, the licensing fees are a significant portion of the initial investment, but in this endeavor there was no such cost."[13] Recently, Orascom has also diversified into a North Korean bank and is active in construction projects such as the Hotel Ryugyŏng, an ambitious but still unfinished 105-floor skyscraper in Pyongyang.

Here is what's smart about Orascom's approach to doing business in North Korea. First, the company negotiated a win-win situation with the government, sometimes going beyond the conventional arrangements in the industry. And second, it followed a strategy of escalating commitments in the country, taking a series of small steps over time as opposed to making a big investment at the beginning. But Orascom was never stubborn or obsessed about succeeding at all costs. In countries in which the business did not evolve according to the initial expectations, the company liquidated its investment. That is what happened, for instance, in Iraq. Orascom invested there in 2003 with the idea of reaping huge rewards once the war came to an end but divested in 2007 in light of poor returns and worse prospects. "The war was never over . . . and we have to invest another $1.25 billion for a new license . . . and I wasn't willing to do that,"[14] explained Sawiris.

Orascom also exited its investments in Jordan and Yemen, and most of the sub-Saharan countries when conditions shifted in ways that made it difficult to make money. But note, too, that Orascom's divestments can hardly be considered failures. For instance, when leaving Iraq, Orascom sold the license for $1.2 billion, for a net gain of $920 million.

Orascom's generally smart and sensible approach to risk taking in emerging economies hasn't been flawless. In Algeria, Orascom's most profitable market, the relationship with the government deteriorated after December 2007 when the company's construction arm sold its Algerian cement business to the French group Lafarge for $12.8 billion without notifying the Algerian government about the deal beforehand. After this diplomatic mistake, the Algerian government levied Orascom for what it claimed were unpaid taxes and further threatened the company with nationalization. Orascom, for its part, has pushed back aggressively, seeking support from both its own Egyptian government and also from the United States on the grounds that American investors hold the majority of the equity of the company.

One U.S. diplomatic cable released by WikiLeaks notes that Alex Shalaby, a "close colleague of Naguib Sawiris, Chairman of Orascom Telecom and an American citizen . . . said Orascom Telecom had already approached the Government of Egypt (GOE) but he was unsure how much the GOE could actually do to help solve the problem . . . Shalaby said he plans to consult with key U.S. investors and may consider requesting U.S. government assistance to help settle the dispute."[15]

However the Algerian dustup turns out, Orascom's hybrid approach to investing in the so-called high-risk countries—one combining proactive negotiations with the government and a defensive strategy of taking small steps—has paid off superbly. Even before the Wind-Vimpelcom deal, Orascom Telecom had 109 million subscribers in 10 countries and was generating $3.825 billion in annual revenue. Orascom has carved out a position for itself in the global mobile telecommunications industry virtually unnoticed. The firm has simply flown under the radar screen of the established multinationals, positioning itself for continued growth while learning along the way how to cope with political risk.

Forging a Way to Global Leadership

Acer and Orascom Telecom give you an accurate taste of what embracing chaos in the new global economy is all about. Let's now turn to India's Bharat Forge, a company whose very reasons for existence are chaos and deprivation. The world's second-largest forging company—after Germany's legendary Thyssenkrupp Forging Group—Bharat Forge has 11 manufacturing locations in Asia (4 in India and 2 in China), Europe (3 in Germany and 1 in Sweden), and the United States (1), where it makes all sorts of metal parts and components such as crankshafts and axle beams for the world's largest automakers, household appliance manufacturers, and other producers of durable goods.

The business of forging dates back seven or eight millennia, which essentially means that it is a mature and technologically stable industry. Forging companies manipulate ferrous or nonferrous metals at different temperatures in order to shape them by pressing, squeezing, or hammering forces. Making metal components through forging provides a number of advantages, such as strength, uniformity, and reliability. Being a supplier to the automotive industry, however, is no fun. Forging companies are under constant pressure to reduce costs and to increase quality levels, design capabilities, and speed of delivery.

The Hindi word *jugaad* is critical to understanding how this Indian enterprise was able to catch the wave of globalization in this ancient industry. Traditionally used to define the art of delivering creative solutions to overcome the lack of resources, jugaad describes an ancestral practice in India, a country handicapped by the lack of resources and infrastructure. Necessity, after all, is the mother of invention, and Bharat Forge provides an excellent example of how jugaad has helped many firms become global players in this new century.

Located in Pune, India, Bharat Forge Limited was incorporated in 1961 and first started forging automotive components

103

in 1966. The company initially focused on the domestic market, with the only recurrent export orders coming from Russian companies in the mid-1980s. As recently as the late 1980s, Bharat Forge was completely unprepared to succeed in international markets. The company simply couldn't meet the requirements of design capabilities, quality, reliability, and speed of delivery associated with the just-in-time manufacturing systems that the Japanese pioneered and the Europeans and Americans were trying to emulate at the time. Moreover, Bharat Forge used outdated equipment and relied extensively on labor rather than machines. The transportation infrastructure around its facilities was so poor that the company had little hope of ever being able to compete on a global basis.

In the spirit of jugaad, however, Baba Kalyani, chairman, managing director, and son of the founder, managed to turn Bharat Forge into "the Infosys of manufacturing."[16] How? For starters, he realized that the company could be a global provider for the automotive industry by taking advantage of India's lower costs. The easy part was to buy state-of-the-art technology to meet global quality standards and to build up scale so as to lower costs even further. Hammers were replaced by automatic forging presses churning out 16,000 tons of forgings per month. Things became more complicated when reorganizing the company to make the most of the new technology, as it required a different type of employee. Blue-collar workers were replaced by white-collar employees capable of using computers for both design and production.

Bharat's decision triggered a series of unplanned—and initially rather chaotic—adaptations that eventually made the company stronger and more competitive. The thousands of new technicians brought in to run the operations could be hired at a much lower cost than in the developed world, allowing the company to introduce multiple process innovations. One of the most remarkable was the so-called maintenance management system.

A mechanized process was designed to minimize downtime—that is, the time during which production is stopped to do maintenance or repair work. Specifically, the system was aimed at anticipating problems in advance. "We feed into the computer, every day and every hour, every piece of data that tells you what you have to do during the manufacturing process, instead of making you deal with the problem during the downtime,"[17] explained Kalyani.

As Bharat's productivity improved, its edge in efficiency started to be acclaimed by its clients. "It is a top-class company," said Wilfried Aulbur, former CEO of Mercedes-Benz India, adding that "We have had good experience and great pricing for the components sourced from them."[18] Even its competitors admire and respect Bharat. "They are always looking for better ways to produce goods,"[19] said Farrokh N. Cooper, chairman and managing director of Cooper Corporation, another Indian forging company.

Once the production process was running smoothly, the next challenge was acquiring new customers, especially outside India, in order to make efficient use of the investments in physical and human capital. That didn't come cheap, but Kalyani was willing to bet big to make the new customers happen. As he once said, "Risks—taking acceptable risks—are part of generating growth."[20] Faced with the disadvantages of its birthplace, Bharat Forge exposed itself to the creative, serendipitous side of risk as the surest way to overcome a vicious cycle of infrastructure deficit, technological backwardness, and lack of international competitiveness. To move forward, the company had to look for new clients, and to facilitate and direct that search, it adopted what was called a "4 × 3 strategy," a growth map based on international expansion (to three regions) and diversification (to up to four main product areas) to make the company less dependent on single clients or industries. The company focused not only on chassis components for commercial cars—its traditional

105

business—but also chassis for passenger cars as well as engine components. It also looked for customers in other industries (the fourth branch of diversification), such as electric power, oil and gas, rail and marine, aerospace, and construction and mining.

On the international front, Bharat Forge's aim was to become a provider to the main clients in these industries in three regions: Europe, the United States, and Asia. Even though this growth strategy entailed risks, it was equally a *derisk* strategy since Bharat Forge became less dependent on single countries and even on single industries while also leveraging its installed capacity and its forging capabilities.

By the end of the 1990s, the strategy of expansion had paid off, and Bharat Forge was exporting to its target triad of Europe, the United States, and Japan, but the company also realized that it would be difficult to keep growing operating just from India. "After turning the business model of manufacturing process upside down and replacing the blue-collar workforce with over 2,000 white-collar staff (with minimum graduate engineering degree), the U.S. market opened up for us from 1992 onward," remembered Kalyani. "By the end of 1999–2000, we had a fairly large volume of exports to every continent, and that's when we started building and getting into global leadership in business. We wanted to be among the top 3–4 companies of the world. For that we needed to be in American, European, and Chinese markets . . . So we began formulating our acquisition strategy. We bought companies which had these customers and turned [them] around."[21]

To enter into the final stage of its growth strategy and overcome once and for all the liability associated with the dire conditions at home, Bharat Forge embarked in a series of global acquisitions. In 2004, Bharat took over Carl Dan Peddinghaus GmbH & Co. KG (CDP), the leading German forging company at the time, with a subsidiary specializing in aluminum forgings. The next year it acquired Sweden's Imatra Kilsta AB, the leading manufacturer of front-axle beams, which included a Scotland-based fully owned subsidiary, Scottish Stampings Ltd. That same year, Bharat Forge gained global reach by acquiring Federal Forge, securing a manufacturing presence in the United States, which is now one of its largest markets. In 2005 the company also established a joint venture in China with FAW Corporation.

These companies gave Bharat not only market share but also technology, as in the case of aluminum forgings. In addition, Bharat Forge raised the value of the acquired companies by applying the best practices generated in the Indian plants. With these acquisitions Bharat Forge became a dual-shore manufacturer—one that can produce with the low-cost advantages of emerging countries but with the design and reliability of developed-country suppliers while also benefiting from a direct contact and access with its main clients, OEMs (original equipment manufacturers) such as Ford, Toyota, and Volkswagen. "It is not possible to develop deep relationships with large OEMs sitting here in India. You need front-end operations in these countries. When a European customer knows that CDP has a low-cost strategy, they will support CDP all the more. Part of the business then gets shifted to India," Kalyani argued.[22]

The quest for new clients also led Bharat Forge to enter into joint ventures aimed at selling nonautomotive forging products. The main partners here are French companies Alstom and Areva and the Indian NTPC Energy Systems. These partners are helping Bharat Forge gain a foothold in forging components for power plants, where it can exploit its manufacturing know-how. Indeed, the nonautomotive business was expected to generate one-third of all company revenues in 2011.

Bharat Forge is not alone among emerging market multinationals that have successfully embraced and neutralized chaos in their favor. Other automotive suppliers are becoming global leaders following a similar blueprint. Consider the case of Wanxiang, China's biggest automotive supplier. Founded in 1969, it initiated foreign growth earlier than Bharat Forge. Once a supplier to big U.S. auto-parts companies like Visteon Corp. and Delphi, Wanxiang used acquisitions in the United States and Europe to expand its product lines and technology base. Many other cases could equally be highlighted here. The low-cost manufacturing skills of emerging market multinationals tend to blend well with the technological capabilities of the targets—a best-of-two-worlds combination.

Inevitably, this type of development makes one wonder why emerging market multinationals are the hunters and not the hunted. Why don't companies from Europe or the United States make acquisitions in emerging economies to pursue this type of strategy? The answer lies in part in the fact that the established automotive suppliers from the rich countries have not reacted well to the ongoing global crisis, in large measure because they were less prepared to face chaotic situations than those in emerging economies. Moreover, as we saw in Chapter 1, this strategy requires attention to detail and excellence at execution, something that emerging market multinationals are much better at doing.

Chaos as Strategy

The stories of Acer, Orascom, Bharat Forge, and many other emerging market multinationals send a powerful message: Growing up rough is not always a disadvantage. In fact, it builds character and can be a clear-cut edge in dealing with chaotic market conditions and still-evolving governmental structures and agencies.

- Because the infrastructure is often spotty at best in their countries of origin, many emerging market multinationals are forced to build and maintain efficient logistics and adopt creative solutions to overcome and/or compensate for the lack of needed resources—a skill set that helps them expand globally, as Bharat Forge illustrates.

- Without ready-made access to capital markets, many emerging market multinationals have had to embrace the risks of expanding internationally with local partners. Acer found it hard to learn how to do it but eventually succeeded very handsomely.

- Forced to find their way through labyrinthine bureaucracies, emerging market multinationals become skilled at proactively negotiating with governments—their own and those of countries they hope to expand into. Orascom Telecom has it all down to a science.

- Having succeeded in extremely difficult situations, emerging market multinationals are loath to give up. On the contrary, they manage to overcome whatever obstacle they face. "When I go anywhere and someone says 'impossible,' I laugh. In 90 percent of the cases, the impossible happens,"[23] said Naguib Sawiris in 2010, reflecting on his experience at the helm of Orascom Telecom Holdings.

Interestingly, in almost all cases these are skills that long-established multinationals once had to develop themselves but have allowed to atrophy. Talking about Telefónica's successful expansion into Latin America, former international chief executive Iñaki Santillana told us, "we have the best ditch-digging technology around [. . .] When it comes to installing a million access lines in record time, no one can beat us."[24] In another interview he argued that in Latin American countries, "we were facing problems of unsatisfied demand that we had solved not long ago in Spain. These problems required short-term project management expertise. North American firms [. . .] were not

FIGURE 4

Learning and profiting from adverse institutional environments.

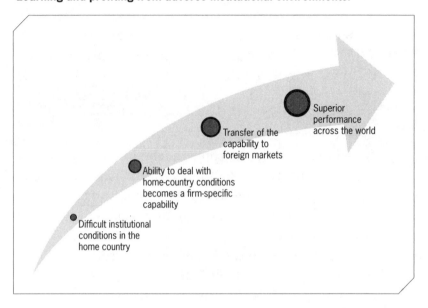

used to installing so many lines at the same time, as their market had become saturated a long time ago."[25]

Figure 4 illustrates the value of recapturing these foundational experiences. Institutionalizing the mindsets born of adverse conditions can lead to superior global performance.

Acquire Smart

Make the most of global bargains.

"It is optimism that is the enemy of the rational buyer."

—WARREN BUFFETT

THE ANNALS OF GLOBAL ACQUISITIONS ARE FILLED WITH failure: megadeals that ended up costing shareholders dearly because of the premium paid, the difficulties at realizing expected synergies, and other postmerger integration issues. While merging balance sheets is straightforward, making two corporate cultures work together is a different story. Many companies have treated acquisitions as ends in themselves, rather than as a means to an end. As Warren Buffett observed, optimism is rampant when a company announces the acquisition of another. The euphoria, however, often ends in disappointment not only because of unwarranted expectations as to the potential benefits but also because of the lack of attention to postacquisition restructuring and integration. Sara Lee famously bought and sold companies without going through the more time-consuming process of improving the management of the acquired assets. Meanwhile, Bimbo, as we have seen, overtook Sara Lee by fixating on operational performance.

The history of acquisitions is not entirely bleak. Established multinationals such as Nestlé, Unilever, and Procter & Gamble have effectively used acquisitions to become not just bigger but more efficient and better serving of their customers. By and large, though, old-line corporate behemoths from developed countries tend to assume a know-it-all attitude toward the companies they acquire and to impose their own hierarchy and culture. They fail to understand that the goal is to learn, not dominate. That was the utterly counterproductive attitude that Ford adopted after acquiring Volvo's car division in 1999 for $6.45 billion. Detroit's number two failed to make the most out of the acquisition, selling it to China's Geely Group for a mere $1.8 billion in 2010.

Geely chairman Li Shufu is determined not to make the same mistake: "After the takeover, Geely remains Geely, and Volvo is still Volvo. The relationship between the two companies is brotherhood and not a parent-and-child relationship."[1]

Ford made similar mistakes after acquiring Jaguar for $2.5 billion in 1989 and Land Rover for $2.7 billion in 2000. After years of mismanagement, Ford sold the companies in 2007 to Tata Motors of India for just $2.3 billion. In both cases, emerging market multinationals were waiting in the wings to take advantage of Ford's failures.

American firms are not alone in thinking they can manage anything they acquire. Ford did not buy Land Rover from its original owner but from Germany's BMW, which had also failed to make good of its own acquisition of the entire Rover group over a period of six years. German automakers are indisputably among the best in the world when it comes to engineering and performance, but acquiring other companies is definitely not their forte. In yet another epic example, Daimler merged in 1998 with Chrysler to form DaimlerChrysler. The deal was valued at a whopping $37 billion. The German side was meant to predominate from the start—and so it did, to the point of stifling Chrysler's ability to compete. After nearly a decade of disappointing results, Daimler sold Chrysler to Cerberus, the private equity group, for $7.4 billion, which in turn passed Chrysler on to Italy's

Fiat in 2009. The deal involved a $12 billion government bailout and a 20 percent equity stake for Fiat in exchange for no cash at all. The Italian firm later raised its stake to almost 54 percent, a serious blow to shareholder value since Fiat did not contribute any new funds. Only time will tell whether the Italians are better than the Germans at managing an acquired company.

So are global acquisitions a bad idea, something to be avoided? Obviously not. While the traditional corporate landscape is littered with failed deals, many of the most high-profile emerging market multinationals have grown more sophisticated and prospered precisely through their acquisitions. Here's the difference: the new multinationals acquire smart—precisely in the two meanings implied. First, they engage in acquisitions to make up for shortcomings in their resources and capabilities, frequently acquiring brands, technologies, or other types of proprietary skills. Second, they choose their targets intelligently, with the intention of advancing their international presence as opposed to making headlines or breaking the record established in a previous megamerger.

Below, case studies of how Tenaris, Cemex, and Tata Communications used smart acquisitions to become leading companies in their respective industries.

Winning Big in Oil Country Tubular Goods

What's the home base of the largest and most sophisticated firm in the cryptic but enormously important industry called "oil country tubular goods"? Germany? Japan or the United States? No. The answer, improbably enough, is Argentina. With a 30 percent share of the global OCTG market and 20 percent of the highly sophisticated market for seamless steel pipes, Tenaris has become one of the world's most admired companies, ahead of competitors such as IPSCO, JFE Holdings, Lone Star

Technologies, and Sumitomo Metal Industries. In 2011, Paolo Rocca, grandson of the founder, received the 2011 Steelmaker of the Year award at the annual Association for Iron & Steel Technology conference held in Indianapolis for "his dynamic and diverse leadership in the manufacturing of steel, most notably for the production of quality pipe and tube to support the world's energy infrastructure."[2]

The origins of Tenaris go back to 1909, when a company then named Dalmine began making steel pipes in Italy. In 1935, Agostino Rocca became managing director. A decade later, Rocca used the experience he had accumulated at Dalmine to launch, along with his son Roberto, a similar enterprise he called Techint. Soon thereafter, father and son moved to Argentina, a chronically unstable country where half of the population came from Italy's poorest regions and the other from Spain's—the only country in the world with such a demographic composition.

In 1954, Agostino founded Siderca, his first company solely devoted to seamless steel tubes, and added that to the Techint portfolio. During the 1960s, 1970s, and 1980s the company suffered through Argentina's endless boom-and-bust cycles, choosing to diversify into related and unrelated industries as a way to cope with uncertainty and chaos. The firm grew into fields such as machinery, engineering, construction, turnkey plant design and construction, oil and gas exploration and production, flat and pressed glass, paper, cement and ceramic tiles, and a bewildering assortment of privatized firms, including sanitary services, railways, toll highways, telecommunications, gas transportation and distribution, power generation, and even correctional facilities. Techint became a true conglomerate.

In the mid-1990s, thanks to the brief period of monetary stability afforded by peso-dollar convertibility, Techint decided to refocus on steel and build a global presence. In 1993 it acquired Mexico's Tamsa, and in 1998 Italy's Dalmine, thus circling back to Techint's own roots. Rechristened DST—from Dalmine, Siderca, and Tamsa—the new company was now the largest OCTG producer in the world. In the following two years it consolidated its leadership position by buying Tavsa in Venezuela and Confab in Brazil. Later, it acquired Maverick Tube Corp. in the United States and Jaya in Indonesia, and in 2011 Brazil's Usiminas. These acquisitions together with joint ventures in Canada, Japan, and China enabled Tenaris to make coiled tubing, drill pipe, pipe casings, and oil pipes in Argentina, Brazil, Canada, Mexico, the United States, Italy, Saudi Arabia, China, Japan, and Indonesia, with service centers in an additional 20 countries. In 2001, DST changed its name to Tenaris, a variation on the Latin word *tenax*, the root of (appropriately enough) *tenacious*. The company is listed on the NYSE as well as in Milan, Buenos Aires, and Mexico City. While incorporated in Luxembourg, its top management and most of its R&D sit in Argentina.

Unlike many companies, Tenaris does not see acquisitions as a raid but as a stepping-stone into profitability. "If we see a target that could enhance our ability to corner a market segment, we will pursue that acquisition," present CEO Paolo Rocca said. "We keep profitability in mind over expansion."[3] Expansion, in fact, proved the way to profitability in the seamless tubing industry in which customers (i.e., oil companies) are increasingly global in their operations and consolidation of producers is rampant because of overcapacity. While Tenaris thought of acquisitions as the way to succeed under such circumstances, its main competitors stayed still. Several of them (IPSCO and Lone Star Technologies, for example) became prey to larger steel companies.

Tenaris's strategy is built on the premise that the company with the most extensive and integrated global network wins.[4] Oil companies are large and global in reach, and they naturally prefer suppliers that have a similar footprint. Historically, they extracted oil directly underneath the ground. With the expansion of global demand and the sharp rise in prices, deeper deposits both onshore and offshore have become the target of exploration and exploitation. That's where Tenaris's seamless steel tubes are crucial. They range from 10 to 14 inches in diameter and can sustain temperatures up to 700 degrees Fahrenheit and pressures up to 12,000 pounds per square inch. "We target customers who are developing and exploring fields that require complex piping," said Rocca. "We can establish clear differentiation and command a large position in these markets—such as nonstandard products developed for deep-water operations off the coast of West Africa, highly corrosive environments in the Caspian Sea, and other high-pressure or high-temperature environments—because there are few competitors."[5]

The secret of Tenaris is its organization and management, especially of acquired companies. "State giveaways are no longer the norm," one executive told us. "Access to cheap credit isn't either. Production technology is not proprietary. Our competitive advantage lies in managing people and processes."

Rocca emphasizes how important it is to integrate acquisitions. "A challenging point for us is being able to manage very different cultures and to adapt and incorporate them into our company. We need to capture brilliant people from diverse cultures. We are establishing an evaluation, training, and promotion system that rewards employee commitment and capability on a worldwide scale. Our people preserve our competitive advantage in the long run," he said, adding, "After our strong expansion in the past few years, this is an opportunity to regroup and strengthen our focus on improving the service we provide our customers worldwide."[6]

The recipe, in truth, is deceptively simple. Strategically, you need acquisitions to create a global presence and serve your customers everywhere they operate. Organizationally, you need to create systems that enable the pieces you acquire to work as one company. But the parent firm must have the capabilities to make the whole system operate as a unit.

Cementing Global Leadership Through Acquisitions

Effective targeting and integration of other companies also enabled Cemex of Mexico to become a leader—one of the world's top five cement firms and number one in certain product categories. The company was founded over a century ago, but most of its international growth has taken place since the mid-1980s through a series of acquisitions, the largest of which was the purchase of Australia's Rinker for $14.2 billion in 2007. Although the global downturn in construction has hit the cement industry hard, Cemex has been able to remain profitable and to service debt through efficiency gains and the disposal of noncore assets.

At first sight, there's nothing particularly special about cement. It's simply a building material that sets and hardens when mixed with water and, when combined with other materials, generically labeled as aggregates, forms a rocklike mass called concrete. Concrete can be mixed on site or sold as a ready-mix by cement manufacturers through mixer trucks. Although its origins can be traced back to the ancient Macedonians almost three millennia ago, modern cement with high standards in terms of setting time and early strength is a product of the Industrial Revolution. That's when one of the most popular variants of the product, Portland cement, was developed using four groups of raw materials: lime, silica, alumina, and iron. Cement is a capital- and energy-intensive industry in which the raw materials are treated in subsequent phases of raw milling, pyro processing, clinker cooling, clinker storage, finish milling, and packing, a series of steps not that different from cooking the raw materials. The cost of a new plant typically equals three years of turnover.

Cement is so heavy relative to its value that it does not pay to transport it by road beyond 200 miles from where it is produced. Not surprisingly, then, the industry was historically very fragmented, with established local or regional companies enjoying hefty profits at the expense of efficiency and innovation. Since the 1980s, however, the increasing availability of low-cost bulk shipping in special cement carriers and the availability of floating cement terminals in ports have transformed the industry as firms with excess capacity gained access to distant markets for the first time. It was an opportunity for firms to build large plants that not only serve the local market but also international markets through sea bulk transportation.

The world's cement leader is Lafarge. Founded in 1833, this French company started its international expansion through foreign direct investment in the 1950s by setting up plants in Canada, Brazil, and North Africa. Beginning in the 1980s, the company grew via acquisition. Nowadays, Lafarge is present in 78 countries. Its main competitors are Holcim of Switzerland, HeidelbergCement of Germany, and Cemex, the first emerging market cement firm to break out of its home territory and today the global leader in ready-mix concrete.

How did Cemex do it? How did it become one of the most widely recognized and respected emerging market multinationals, famous for its ability to grow through acquisitions and widely considered by industry consultants to be Lafarge's superior when it comes to integrating acquisitions? Maybe the roots lie in the fact that Cemex itself was the result of a sometimes rocky 1931 merger between two Mexican cement manufacturers, Cementos Hidalgo (founded in 1906) and Cementos Portland Monterrey, founded in 1920 by Lorenzo H. Zambrano, grandfather of Lorenzo Zambrano, the current CEO of Cemex.

Despite his pedigree, Zambrano's path to the CEO position was far from smooth. A generation earlier, other shareholding families had pushed for a professional manager, Jesús Barrera. Over time Barrera also became an important shareholder and was succeeded by his own son, Rodolfo. The Barreras grew the company in Mexico by building new plants and acquiring other companies, like Cementos Maya, Cementos Portland del Bajío, and Cementos Guadalajara. With the acquisition of the latter in 1976, Cemex became the Mexican market leader. Then, in 1985, the time came to replace Barrera, and the board turned to Zambrano as its new CEO.

An engineer educated in the prestigious Mexican University ITESM (popularly known as Tecnológico de Monterrey), Zambrano had joined the company in 1968, after getting an MBA from Stanford. His relation was never good with Barrera, who intended for his own son to succeed him, but Zambrano was determined to reach the top position. In fact, he became so devoted to Cemex that he never married. Working in the operations department, he spent a lot of time studying how to integrate IT into the management of the company, especially to monitor plant performance. When he finally was appointed CEO, IT was one of the cornerstones of his efforts to turn around the company. His two other key ideas were to make all decisions on the basis of the value created for the customer *and* to grow aggressively via acquisitions. Zambrano also opted for focusing on cement as the core business, divesting noncore assets.

One of the first future-shaping decisions Zambrano made was to create an IT department and to introduce the position of CIO. "At that point, there was no IT department. Basically, there were a couple of computers that ran accounting programs. We realized that IT needed to be a key part of our new business strategy,"[7] said José Luis Luna, Cemex's current CIO. The company invested heavily in IT infrastructure, creating CemexNET, a satellite communications system that interconnected all of their plants, and set up GPS tracking on all of its trucks. The more established European and American competitors never thought about that. Later Cemex created an Internet platform to build B2B portals to connect suppliers, distributors, and customers. This infrastructure led the company to redefine working processes with the help of IT. This was a huge internal revolution that boosted efficiency inside the company in more ways than one, perhaps most dramatically in terms of customer service.

In a typical show of managerial prowess, the company, now in full control of production and delivery systems and in direct contact with customers, started to guarantee delivery of its products in just *20 minutes*. That was the central reason why Cemex became number one in the world in ready-mix concrete. Cemex also improved the value proposition for its customers by discovering new market opportunities. Mexico is among the 15 largest countries both in terms of cement production and consumption, and one peculiarity of the market is that a large segment is comprised of individual customers who buy the cement in bags. In order to serve them better, Cemex set up a chain of building-materials distributors named Construrama. This network was a long-term cooperation project with existing Mexican distributors that, in exchange for exclusivity in selling only Cemex cement, received technical, management, and marketing support, and the right to use the label Construrama. Nowadays more than 2,000 stores are associated with the chain.

Cemex also innovated by launching Patrimonio Hoy, a savings-and-loan program that helps low-income citizens build and expand their homes by making access to cement blocks and other building materials affordable. Again, none of the European or American competitors made similar moves.

These initiatives embedded Cemex's leadership in the Mexican market, which it came to fully dominate after acquiring Cementos Tolteca in 1989, the second-largest cement producer in the country. Creating value with acquisitions is all about buying a company at a discount price and/or raising its capacity to increase profits. Cemex put the emphasis on the latter. Given the myriad inefficient cement producers around the world, the industry was full of consolidation opportunities. Armed with its superior IT system and excellent skills at customer relationships, Cemex went on a shopping spree, buying competitors in Spain, Venezuela, Panama, Dominican Republic, Colombia, Costa Rica, the Philippines, Egypt, and the United States.

To avoid indigestion, Cemex moved quickly to integrate the acquired firms. It created a team of managers that would descend upon each acquired company to transfer all of Cemex's expertise, technology, and systems, and then move onto the next acquisition. Over time the company learned to shorten the process of turning around and transferring its management routines and systems. Whereas the integration of the Spanish plants took two years, 10 years later the same process took only two months. "It's like a SWAT team. For the first two months, we look for quick hits that will bring immediate savings,"[8] said one experienced leader of these teams. But this process was not a mere unilateral transfer of systems and routines. On the contrary, Cemex also looked for sound managerial practices in the acquired companies to adopt. "We introduce our system, but we also pick up good practices that we haven't seen anywhere else," this same leader pointed out.[9]

In 2000, already a big global player, Cemex launched an ambitious program that took stock of what was learned during the growth process and used this as the basis for establishing a set of principles and values for managing the company. This program, dubbed the Cemex Way, aims to disseminate and identify best practices across the whole corporation, standardizing business processes with the help of Cemex's IT infrastructure. "Essentially, it is internal benchmarking,"[10] explained Zambrano. The program also fostered innovation by encouraging employees to propose innovations.

The Cemex Way was introduced just as Cemex started a second wave of acquisitions that included bigger targets. Its first prey was Southdown, the second-largest cement company in the United States. Southdown was a tough test for company principles and practices. Not only was it by far the largest target Cemex had sought to acquire and integrate, Southdown also operated in a market in which bulk sales to firms were much more important than sales to individuals. Rather than make the acquisition fit the Cemex Way, however, Cemex altered the "way" after the U.S. experience.

Besides other acquisitions of regional players since 2000, two deals have been critical in the recent development of Cemex. The first was the 2005 $5.8 billion acquisition of Britain's RMC, a company with a presence in 20 additional countries and equal in size to Cemex. That integration process involved 400 managers from Cemex being sent to the different RMC plants to implement the benchmarking philosophy of the Cemex Way. The success of this integration led Zambrano to make an even bolder move: the acquisition of Australia's Rinker, a company with a strong presence in the United States, for a whopping $14.2 billion.

The latter deal was met by board resistance, so Cemex had to offer an important premium for the acquisition, adding much debt to the company's balance sheet. Worse, this acquisition was made just one year before the 2008 financial crisis, which slowed down the demand for cement in the developed world. Cemex's finances deteriorated steeply enough that in 2009 it was forced to sell the Australian operations of Rinker to Holcim, its Swiss competitor.

Reflecting on those tough years, Zambrano said that "The mistake was not to finance the Rinker acquisition more conservatively," but, he added, "If every time we make a decision to grow, we think of the absolute worst that can happen, then you don't do anything."[11] Besides, his company was far from the only one in the industry doing financial restructuring in the wake of the Great Recession. World leader Lafarge has also been forced to refinance its debt.

The bottom line is that, even in perilous times, Cemex is still on a growth path. In 2010, the company launched Blue Rock Cement Holdings with the aim of investing in the cement industry in growing markets. Cemex holds a minority equity position (with the option to acquire Blue Rock's assets) and provides management expertise. So far, Blue Rock has invested in Peru. Cemex is also looking for targets in India and China, where its competitors Lafarge and Holcim are already present, but is obviously reluctant to pay big premiums for local firms. In fact, the company recently declined the acquisition of a company in India because of its high valuation.

Cemex offers a key lesson to would-be acquirers, especially when having a global consolidation purpose in mind. Don't buy anything unless you have the skills to turn the target around. You can't win the acquisition game without developing a set of routines for making the target more efficient and integrating it with the rest of your operations. Obviously, not all of Cemex's acquisitions were equally successful. But even in the case of Rinker, the only mistake was not to anticipate the magnitude of the current financial crisis, something that hardly anyone in the world did. The ability of Cemex to turn around cement companies remains intact, and Zambrano is still thinking of further acquisitions. In his own words: It is "within our DNA."[12]

Wiring the World through Acquisitions

Acquisitions turned Tata Communications into not only the world's largest international wholesale voice carrier—over 40 billion minutes annually, or about 10 percent of the world total—but also the most efficient. Tata owns a submarine and terrestrial cable network of more than 146,000 miles, nearly six times the length of the equator; a tier-1 IP network with connectivity to more than 200 countries and territories; and a huge data center in Pune, India, offering co-location, hosting, and storage services for customers.

Tata Communications, of course, is part of the Tata conglomerate, founded by Jamsetji Nusserwanji in 1868. Comprising over 100 companies and employing some 330,000 people, its revenues top $84 billion across such a diverse assortment of industries as consumer goods, chemicals, cement, steel, automobiles, engineering, energy, information systems, telecommunications, financial services, hospitality, and many, many others. It is now under the leadership of the family's fifth generation. *The Economist* estimated Tata's return on equity as of the year ending in March 2011 at an astounding 25 percent, the highest of any Indian conglomerate. Scale, scope, political connections, and true managerial capabilities all play a role in this company's competitive position.[13]

The Tata Group made several acquisitions in telecommunications within the compressed time period of one decade: VSNL and Dishnet DSL in India, Teleglobe in Canada, Tyco Global Network in the United States, Neotel in South Africa, and Cipris in France, among others. In 2008, Tata grouped its telecommunications companies under Tata Communications. In addition to the physical infrastructure, Tata gained access to other valuable assets with these acquisitions. For instance, Teleglobe came with a software system that facilitates the location of roaming mobile phones used by 95 percent of telecom operators in the world.

A key moment in Tata's foray into telecommunications came with the 2002 acquisition of 45 percent of VSNL, the state-owned monopoly on international long-distance voice. Once in the Tata fold, the company became the target of an extensive acculturation program.

"It wasn't easy," former CEO Srinath Narasimhan said about dealing with the bureaucracy at the formerly state-owned telecom monopoly. "There was simply no atmosphere of empowerment. Typically, what people would write on a file would be: 'This is what I think we should do but my boss may please give his opinion.' The file would go through 17 signatures on the way before it came to me. Then I'd have people who came saying, 'I know I have the authority, but I just wanted your opinion.' I'd simply say: 'Not going to get it. Back to you.'"[14]

Acquiring the behemoth was the easy part. Making it work as a customer-oriented company was much harder. "We rewrote everything from scratch," Narasimhan continued, "right from goal setting to assessment systems. And then a large chunk of people—almost a thousand—opted for voluntary retirement." Maybe the greatest long-term value of acquiring VSNL lay in the very experience Narasimhan describes. By learning how to deal with a fossilized state-owned organization in its own backyard, Tata Communications was preparing itself for making similar acquisitions abroad since most state-owned companies share common features.

We've already seen in the cases of Tenaris and Cemex that the true value of an acquisition to the acquirer depends on what happens after the deal is done. An illuminating example of this dynamic is Tata's acquisition of Tyco Global Network in the United States from the storied Switzerland-incorporated, New Jersey-based conglomerate Tyco International. The deal was managed by Kishor Chaukar, Tata Industries Managing Director. In 2005 he told a reporter that "the price that VSNL has paid is a fraction of Tyco's total cable assets. It is a unique global network, with assets of almost \$2.5 billion," adding that "VSNL was short on bandwidth, information, and technology. With this deal no one will be able to beat us."[15]

In telecommunications, customers expect seamless global services. The VSNL acquisition served that purpose as well. "This agreement will allow us to provide our enterprise and carrier clients with customized and robust connectivity solutions under one trusted global brand," said Dave Ryan, chief operations officer at VSNL America.[16] But seamless services don't just happen: Any such strategy of growth through acquisition requires strong postmerger integration skills to succeed.

Indiscriminate integration simply won't work. As experienced acquirers know, the trick consists in realizing what needs to be integrated and what does not. "We avoided the trap of 'let's integrate everything' when it came to VSNL, VSNL International, and Teleglobe,"[17] noted Srinivasa Addepalli, head of strategy at Tata Communications. Unifying the brand should and could wait, but the synergies from creating a single global operating unit to capitalize on scale, reduce costs, and manage traffic were absolutely essential for the acquisition to pay off.

In order to better appreciate Tata Communications' success, compare its international acquisition strategy with those of BellSouth and AT&T. At the height of its Latin American influence during the 1990s, BellSouth overintegrated in some areas and underintegrated in others, forcing the company to eventually sell its assets to Telefónica of Spain. And that was only the beginning of its problems: BellSouth also expanded into one region only—a kind of antiglobalism when the world was headed in exactly the opposite direction—and it primarily simply wanted to milk the assets it had acquired. "We are not really committing new money to that region," said CEO Duane Ackerman in 2003, "but we're managing what we've got."[18]

AT&T had its own disastrous bout with thinking too small. The company decided to focus on corporate customers, a segment that is increasingly global, without establishing a global presence of its own. AT&T's CEO Bob Allen also caused the company to lose billions because of his strategic flip-flopping, which made it impossible to allocate enough resources to its telecommunications business. The 1991 purchase of NCR Corp. for $7.5 billion as a way to enter the computer business was especially disastrous because it distracted AT&T's management from the new opportunities in global telecommunications being created by deregulation and technological innovation.

Whether you are selling steel tubes like Tenaris, cement like Cemex, or telecommunication services like Tata, if you want to be a global player, with global customers, you must blanket the world, and you must be willing to spend the resources, time, and effort to integrate your acquired assets so that you add value to your customers. Acquiring bits and pieces scattered throughout the world with no connectivity or integration among them will not be helpful to global customers.

BellSouth and AT&T also both paid far too much attention to their stock price. They did not pursue acquisitions hard enough because they feared investors. Yes, in the short run, an acquirer's value in the stock market almost always suffers, but if the acquisition strategy is well executed, the market will reward the acquirer in the long term. Neither BellSouth nor AT&T's managers and owners had the patience. Tata Communications, as a member of the Tata group of companies, was shielded from this type of investor pressure and managerial short-term orientation, an advantage that many emerging market multinationals possess thanks to their ownership structure. Few of them have widely dispersed share ownership. They are mostly owned by families or controlled by the state. While these types of owners have priorities (and challenges) of their own, they tend to focus on long-term profitability rather than short-term gains.

In making acquisitions, Tata Communications has gained yet another advantage relative to established multinationals. While offering global connectivity at a low cost, the company is stronger in emerging economies than in developed ones. That, too, could be a big plus. "The next trillion dollars to be made in global communications," observed Camille Mendler, vice president of research at Yankee Group, "will depend heavily on emerging markets, where Tata Communications is already a leading player."[19]

Acquiring Your Way to the Top

Cross-border acquisitions are the fastest way to gain global scale and expand quickly into foreign markets. Indeed, for latecomer firms, they are often the *only* way to get into the top positions in the global rankings. That said, many otherwise smart companies have dug their own grave because of failed acquisitions. Swept up by the chase and their own hubris, and perhaps impatient to make a bold move, they go to sometimes insane extremes to outbid competitors, convinced they can turn a profit no matter the price paid. Just as bad, that same arrogance tells them that the acquired company has everything to learn from the acquirer, and the acquirer nothing to learn from the acquired. Instead of asking how can we best work together and what can we learn from one another, the message delivered is "My way or the highway."

The recipe for *successful* acquisitions requires several ingredients. The first is to set a clear goal for the acquisition, namely, global consolidation and/or learning. Emerging market multinationals have excelled at both, as the cases discussed in this chapter illustrate. The other ingredients involve choosing the right target, at the right price, at the right time, and with the right integration approach. Failing to meet *any* of these requirements can seriously compromise the growth plan of the company. Figure 5 highlights these critical factors for making smart acquisitions:

- First, acquire what you really need, and don't be afraid of the size of the target, especially when the acquisition helps fill internal gaps. Think about the bold acquisitions made by Geely (Volvo) and the Indian steel giant Mittal, which purchased Europe's Arcelor in 2006 for a whopping $33.1 billion. No matter whether you want to gain size or secure entry into a new market or field, always try to stand on the shoulder of giants.
- Second, choose the right time. Making bold acquisitions does not necessarily entail paying big premiums. The volatility of global competition ensures that good targets will eventually become available, at bargain prices. But in order to take advantage of the opportunities, you must be prepared—financially and organizationally—to make your move.
- Finally, choose the right integration mode. Depending on the aim of the acquisition—global consolidation or

FIGURE 5

Critical factors in aquiring smart.

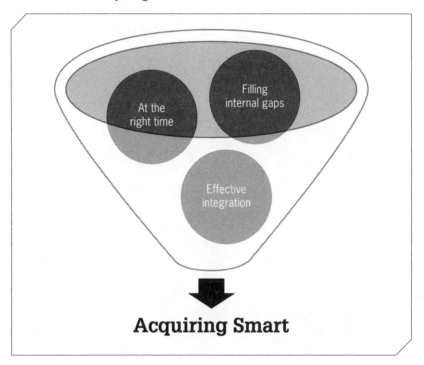

At the right time

Filling internal gaps

Effective integration

Acquiring Smart

learning—the target must be either fully integrated or granted autonomy in decision making. Gains from experiential learning should never be neglected. The best example is the Cemex Way, which established a philosophy of benchmarking and innovation throughout the entire corporation. Also never forget that, especially when acquiring to consolidate, the bidder needs to be able to transfer some management capabilities to the target in order to create value. Acquisitions are not a miraculous solution for firms lacking capabilities. As Cemex's CEO Lorenzo Zambrano once said, "If we cannot grow in markets where we already are, we cannot grow."[20]

Expand with Abandon

If you wait until you're ready,
you've waited too long.

"Impossible is a word to be found only in the dictionary of fools."

— NAPOLEON BONAPARTE

IN THE OLD WORLD DOMINATED BY ONE LARGE ECONOMY and predictable patterns of technology development, production, and trade, companies approached the process of international expansion in a very orderly three-part minuet.

First, aspiring multinationals ventured abroad only after ensuring that their organization was ready for such a momentous move. They thought about foreign markets as steps in a ladder, with the easiest ones coming first and the more distant, harder ones coming last. Thus, for American firms Britain was easier to enter than Germany, and Mexico was more of a natural market to explore than Brazil. And many companies didn't even dare compete in Japan—too hard a market to crack. As they entered foreign markets by moving up this hierarchy of difficulty, they would look down toward their home country and often experience a profound sense of vertigo.

Even after they had determined to invade distant shores, these companies calibrated their foreign-market entry strategies in terms of years, if not decades. McDonald's needed a half century to generate more sales abroad than in the United States. Granted, the United States is a huge market with plenty of room for internal expansion, but consider the case of Sweden's H&M, the world's most valuable clothing brand. Even with the comparatively modest opportunities for internal expansion presented by its home country, H&M waited 17 years after its founding in 1947 to enter its first foreign country—and that was Norway! Not until its fifty-third year did H&M venture across the Atlantic to the United States. Even today, the firm has a tiny presence in Asia and virtually none in Latin America.

By contrast, Spain's Zara (owned by Inditex), the world's largest clothing retailer and the second most valuable brand, has opened stores in over 80 countries, most within the past 10 years. The pioneer of fast fashion thinks in terms of months, if not weeks, when it comes to foreign markets. We saw in previous chapters that Acer, Samsung, and Suzlon were also impatient when it came to global expansion—and their bargain has paid off handsomely. Acer is now the number two global personal computer brand, Samsung the leading consumer electronics firm, and Suzlon one of the top wind-turbine manufacturers.

Finally, even after entering foreign markets, old-line multinationals tended to escalate their commitment of resources slowly, starting with exports, then with a warehouse, and later adding a plant or two. To be sure, there's a certain wisdom in such a cautious approach: the firm and its managers have time to learn and warm up to the idea of operating across a large number of markets. But waiting too long to feel good about foreign expansion is a luxury most firms simply cannot afford in the new global economy of the twenty-first century.

In this chapter, we look at three leading emerging market multinationals that turned the traditional blue-chip expansion minuet into something closer to a frenzied jitterbug—and lived to tell the story: China's BYD, one of the largest rechargeable-battery manufacturers and a firm with the potential of creating the first fully competitive electric car; telecommunications giant América Móvil, which has made owner Carlos Slim the wealthiest person on the planet; and India's Ocimum Biosolutions, which expanded without pause to become one of the top-rated genomics outsourcing companies.

Who Will Be the World's Largest Automaker?

In 2008, a full two years before Toyota and General Motors launched the hybrid plug-in Prius and the Chevy Volt, China's BYD stunned the world with the first mass-market electric hybrid plug-in car, cryptically called the F3DM (for dual mode). That same year, MidAmerican Energy Holdings acquired a 10 percent stake in the firm for $230 million. MidAmerican's majority owner, Warren Buffett, argued that BYD "has a shot at becoming the world's largest automaker, primarily by selling electric cars, as well as a leader in the fast-growing solar power industry."[1] Far from hyperbolic, this statement merely reflects the widely shared prediction by industry experts that electric cars will be the dominant form of transportation before we know it. And the most expensive and sophisticated component in an electric car is, well, the battery.

Wang Chuanfu founded BYD in 1995 in Shenzen, the tiny fishing village near Hong Kong that transformed itself into the world's leading manufacturing hub. Trained as a chemist and formerly a government researcher, Wang set out to compete against Sony, Sanyo, and Matsushita in the rechargeable battery industry. He started by focusing on customers making low-cost computers and mobile phones. By 2002, his company was one of the four largest battery makers and, by 2008, the world's largest manufacturer of nickel-cadmium batteries, capturing more than half of the global mobile-phone battery market. That's over 500 million batteries a year!

The company has grown at 45 percent for each of the past five years. In 2010 BYD topped the Bloomberg Businessweeek Tech 100 list of the fastest-growing technology companies. Today, it supplies Apple with the lithium-ion batteries for the iPad and iPhone. You get the picture: lightning speed of expansion while constantly improving production methods and product quality. Otherwise, Apple and Nokia would not continue sourcing their batteries from BYD.

In addition to focusing on execution and building up scale faster than anyone else, BYD innovated. First, the company figured that automating battery production was more expensive than using manual labor, especially when product cycles are very short and product specifications change fast. Retooling costs are just too high when compared with the versatility of the human factor. Instead of buying expensive robots from Japan, Wang decided to hire tens of thousands of employees from rural China.

Second, BYD developed a technology for making batteries at ambient temperature as opposed to in expensive heated dry rooms. This enabled them to make lithium-ion batteries—more powerful than nickel-cadmium ones—as cheap as $12, down from $40. While this innovation definitely undermines BYD's capabilities and strength in the nickel-cadmium battery market, it also provides the company with a huge advantage relative to other firms in the present and going forward, given that more than two-thirds of the global market is now accounted for by lithium-ion rechargeable batteries. BYD could have enjoyed its dominant position in the nickel-cadmium battery market, milking the profits from their investment, but it knew better. Wang and his team realized customers would eventually embrace the higher-performing batteries, so they invested heavily in the new technology even at the risk of destroying competence in the older one.

BYD also pursued related diversification by entering the mobile-phone business itself as a component maker and original-equipment manufacturer for companies such as Nokia and

Motorola. BYD Electronic, the subsidiary created in 2002 to manage this line of business, has eight factories in China and one each in India, Hungary, and Romania. In effect, this amounts to a worldwide solution in an industry that requires just-in-time production and delivery of rapidly changing products and designs. Bottom line: if you don't build a global presence fast, you're out of the game.

After coming to dominate the world of batteries in little over a decade, Wang needed to find another challenge, so in 2003, BYD spent $393 million to acquire a 77 percent stake in a derelict state-owned automaker called Qinchuan Automobile Company. By 2010, BYD Automobile Co. Ltd. was the sixth-largest firm in the world's fastest-growing automobile market, selling nearly 500,000 cars, and starting exports to Africa, South America, and the Middle East. The company can't wait to sell to Europe and the United States, though the Great Recession has thrown some cold water over its plans.

BYD's main automobile assembly operations are in the city of Xi'an, one of China's four ancient capitals and home to the world-famous terra-cotta warriors. The company is contemplating assembly operations in other emerging economies, to improve market access and tap into other pools of talent. Automobile battery research and development, however, is based in Shenzhen, next to the main battery facilities, where about 5,000 automobile engineers work together with as many battery engineers. Even in this wirelessly interconnected world, nothing fosters innovation better than engineers interacting with one another down the hallway.

Wang's vision is to move away from gasoline-powered cars—in part because of BYD's experience in batteries but also because competition in the electric car industry is less intense, at least for now. In addition, an electric car is easier to manufacture thanks to the smaller number of components—about 210 primary parts versus 1,400. "It's almost hopeless for a latecomer like us to compete with GM and other established automakers with a century of experience in gasoline engines," Wang observed. "With electric vehicles, we're all at the same starting line."[2] Herein lies a key lesson that has been the road to success for multiple emerging market multinationals. Embraer, Haier, and now BYD chose a product, a segment, or a technology they could learn fast and use as a stepping-stone into a larger, more profitable family of products, segments, and/or technologies.

Judging from their actions, established automobile companies concur with Wang's assessment that BYD is uniquely positioned to take the electric vehicle market by storm. Daimler, the prestigious and all-powerful German company, is seeking to partner with BYD to develop electric vehicles. In 2011, the legendary German automaker obtained authorization from the Chinese government to form a joint venture with its youthful Chinese counterpart. "Our new joint venture is well positioned to make the most of the vast potential of electric mobility in China," said Daimler CEO Dieter Zetsche. "We've now had the green light to move ahead—and are especially pleased to receive the business license just a few months after signing the contract. It will accelerate our joint efforts to create an all-new electric vehicle for the Chinese market."[3] The joint venture plans to launch the new car by 2013. "Daimler and BYD will take full advantage of each other's specialized expertise to develop a brand-new electric vehicle in line with the government's policies to build a greener future," said Ulrich Walker, CEO of Daimler Northeast Asia.[4] For BYD, partnering with Daimler in fewer than eight years after entering the industry is like a dream come true. It is also tangible proof of BYD's success at finding a competitive position in the global marketplace with a high potential for growth and profitability.

Building a global leader in rechargeable batteries from scratch in just over a decade and entering the big leagues of the automobile industry has earned Wang a reputation for tenacity, innovation, and boldness. "This guy is a combination of Thomas Edison and Jack Welch," said Charlie Munger, Buffett's longtime partner, "something like Edison in solving technical problems, and something like Welch in getting done what he needs to do. I have never seen anything like it."[5] The future of electric automobiles is far from settled, but BYD's track record, brief as it is, gives the company a serious head start over conventional car companies struggling to keep up with technological developments in this new field. Indeed, BYD is one of the best textbook examples of leapfrogging over established players.

Shaping the Digital Future, One Cell Phone at a Time

América Móvil is another good example of expansion and growth at the speed of light. Although this company has mastered the art of making acquisitions, the hallmark of its international expansion has been speed, whether in marketing innovation, expansion through acquisitions, or diversification into unrelated industries. Indeed the company's trajectory is almost as spectacular as that of its founder, Carlos Slim, the world's richest man, with an estimated net worth of $69 billion, as of March 2012, according to *Forbes* magazine.[6]

The son of a Lebanese immigrant to Mexico who became the successful owner of a retail business in the country's capital, Slim was educated as an engineer and briefly practiced that profession. In 1965, at age 25, he shifted his career to business, taking the initial steps for building what today is the Grupo Carso Holding. Slim's first business endeavors included launching a brokerage company, getting into the real estate business, and acquiring a bottling company. Later, he launched still more ventures and acquired companies across virtually every sector of the economy, from construction to trading, and from tobacco to mining.

Instead of being a liability, the volatility of the Mexican economy played into Slim's hands during this impressive growth spurt by offering him multiple opportunities to acquire distressed companies. For instance, in 1982, after the sharp devaluation of the peso, Slim bought several Mexican subsidiaries of U.S. multinationals sold on the cheap by their parent companies, which only wanted to get rid of them. "These were the best times ever," Slim remembered. "Nobody wanted to buy anything and everyone wanted to sell."[7] Slim did not just buy anything, however. He was only interested in companies that generated huge amounts of cash flow, so each acquisition generated resources for the next.

In 1990, two critical events took place. First, Slim took Grupo Carso Holding public. Then the company entered into an alliance with Southwestern Bell and France Télécom to bid for the privatization of the Mexican national telecommunications monopoly, Telmex. The deal was extremely advantageous because Telmex was being packaged with two bonus concessions. One was a six-year monopoly on long-distance calls. The other was the true gem: the sole license for cellular telecommunications covering the entire country. The license had been previously granted to DIPSA, the Telmex subsidiary that commercialized cellular services under the Telcel brand, and transferred as part of the privatization package that Slim and his partners bought. This was a huge deal by any standard—and a great handout some would say.

No matter how advantageous the deal was for Slim, he made the company grow like no other bidder could have done. Telecommunications in Mexico in 1990 was an underdeveloped industry in a developing country, with low penetration rates and obsolete technologies. At that time, DIPSA had only 35,000 subscribers in a country of 84 million. To capitalize on the situation, Slim decided to move quickly before the privileges he had managed to obtain were taken away. He invested heavily in infrastructure, eliminating the waiting list for new telephone lines. In addition, Slim adopted an aggressive strategy to commercialize mobile phones: selling prepaid cards packaged with subsidized terminals. While nowadays this is a widespread strategy, Slim was the pioneer in realizing that a successful emerging market telecom company in the digital age could not target only high-income customers. Randall Stephenson, presently the CEO of AT&T, was sent to Mexico in 1992 by Southwestern Bell to work at Telmex. Reflecting on the events of the period, he observed that "You have very few opportunities in life where it is just grow, grow, grow."[8] Such growth allowed Telmex to preempt the competition in wireless telecommunications.

Slim isn't afraid to play hardball or milk his advantages. In landlines, for example, Telmex did not exactly ingratiate itself with market watchdogs. One controversial issue has to do with the high price charged to other operators using its network to complete a call. In fact, a recent study by the Organization for Economic Cooperation and Development, of which Mexico is a member, clearly documents that to this day Mexican consumers pay monopoly prices for fixed and wireless telecommunications and for Internet access.

By the mid-1990s, with growth opportunities in the Mexican market diminishing, Slim began looking abroad, as a way of taking advantage of the great cash flows generated in Mexico. In 1995, just five years after buying Telmex, he began developing projects to enter into the United States and other Latin American countries. Then, in 2000, the company made its great leap forward in the international arena by splitting the wireless business into a separate entity, América Móvil, and adding to it cable TV (Cablevisión) and other international activities previously carried out by Telmex in Guatemala, Puerto Rico, Brazil, Ecuador, Argentina, and the United States.

Even though telecommunications liberalization and privatization were well advanced in Latin America by then, the timing proved perfect for hitting the fast lane. At that time, many U.S.

companies had still not got the knack of the Latin American markets and were hurt by the burst of the tech bubble at home, so they were more than willing to sell their investments in Latin America to generate cash. And that is when América Móvil purchased all or part of the Latin American assets of France Télécom, AT&T, Verizon, Telecom Italia Mobile, BellSouth, Bell Canada, and Southwestern Bell Corporation International. The latter two companies partnered with América Móvil for its international activities until 2002, when they withdrew, unable to keep up with the rapid investment pace set by América Móvil.

As a latecomer with plenty of cash, marketing expertise and operating know-how, América Móvil easily outpaced its competitors. It capitalized on the expertise accrued in Mexico and spread that knowledge throughout Latin America. In some cases, established telecoms had invested in older technologies that became obsolete. América Móvil left those dinosaurs in the dust by adopting the most advanced technology, the GSM standard, in the countries it served. As the company gained scale, learning, and speed, it used its always-aggressive acquisition policy to cement a new competitive edge. América Móvil is now present in the United States, Mexico, Guatemala, El Salvador, Nicaragua, Honduras, Panama, Puerto Rico, Dominican Republic, Jamaica, Colombia, Ecuador, Peru, Brazil, Chile, Argentina, Paraguay, and Uruguay, in most cases under the Claro brand. (*Claro* for "clear," just what you want a telecommunications hookup to be.) Whatever you call it, though, América Móvil is the telecommunications leader in Latin America, with (as of December 2010) a total of 276.5 million accesses—wireless lines, landlines, and other services such as pay TV. Compare that with runner-up Spain's Telefónica, which competes under the Movistar brand. As of the same date, Telefónica had 183.7 million accesses in Latin America, almost 100 million fewer than América Móvil, although the Spanish company claims a total of 287.6 accesses worldwide.

In fact, a comparison between the two telecommunications titans is interesting. Because it got into international expansion later than the Spanish company, América Móvil benefited from low-cost acquisitions, while Telefónica's initial investment took place at an earlier time when optimistic profit expectations invited bidders to pay huge premiums for operating licenses. To Telefónica's credit, though, the company has adapted much better than U.S. telecoms to the Latin American markets and is competing fiercely against América Móvil across the whole continent. One example: Telefónica acquired the international operations of BellSouth and is switching to the GSM technology across the region. The main battlefield now is in Brazil, the largest Latin American country, where after several acquisitions both companies are competing —as happens in other countries—with integrated packages of voice, data, and TV telecommunication services.

Even though there is still room for growth in telecommunications in Latin America, opportunities to grow by buying on the cheap are fading, not only in Latin America but throughout the developed world, with the exception of Europe, where the crisis of the euro allowed América Móvil to take a controlling stake in Holland's KPN and to increase its stake in Telekom Austria to 23 percent. Perhaps for this reason, Carso, the holding company that controls América Móvil, is diversifying outside the telecommunications industry throughout Latin America. Explaining his future plans in Colombia, Carlos Slim said that "The government is actively looking at the development of the oil industry and is promoting other investments . . . We're looking at what to do beyond the telecommunications business that we've been building for 10 years in Colombia."[9] The moral: when the core business of your company is finding fast-growth opportunities, lacking industry experience is hardly a barrier. At least, this is the lesson that emerges from the wild ride of Carlos Slim on his way to becoming the world's richest man. Industry experience can be provided by established partners, but the hard part is to have ready the cash flows and appropriate strategies for developing and implementing successful growth plans. To date, Slim's track record seems virtually flawless.

Pioneering the Offshore Lab

If electric automobiles and mobile telecommunications don't strike you as good enough examples of the imperative of speed when it comes to global expansion, consider bioinformatics, one of the key growth industries in the brave new world of the twenty-first century.

New drug development used to be a hit-or-miss process. Until the early 1970s, researchers at government, university, and corporate labs would inject rats displaying some pathology with hundreds of chemical compounds, hoping to find one that would ameliorate the symptoms or cure the disease. No wonder the process was called "drug discovery," not drug invention. It was somewhat akin to positioning a million monkeys at a million typewriters, hoping to produce a perfect Shakespearean sonnet.

Advances in physiology and biochemistry enabled researchers to come up with drugs specifically designed to inhibit or exacerbate certain biological mechanisms thought to be related to the pathology. Drug discovery gave way to drug design. Also in the 1970s, the field of genomics took off. By 2001, the Human Genome Project was completed, and by 2007 the entire human genetic sequence was mapped. Genomics promises to help researchers identify more cellular or molecular structures involved in the pathology of interest. Those structures can then be used as targets for drug-design efforts. The various pieces needed to revolutionize pharmaceutical innovation were thus in place. All that was needed was entrepreneurs to put them together.

Both genomics research and drug design require extensive use of bioinformatics, or the application of information technology and statistics to biomedical research. This is how companies in India have come to play a prominent role in the global pharmaceutical industry. Columbus found the Americas while aiming at India, and pharmaceutical firms found India's formidable skills at information technology while trying to use genomics to find new drugs.

Bioinformatics has developed very quickly to include all sorts of arcane—though very useful—tools, including various kinds of algorithms, artificial intelligence, circuit theory, computation theory, data mining, discrete mathematics, image processing, signal processing, simulation, software engineering, systems theory, and web technologies, among many others. Indian engineers and programmers are among the best versed and most affordable in each of those fields. Hence, the market for genomics outsourcing is booming, especially on the subcontinent.

Back in the late 1990s, Anu Ancharya became keenly aware of these shifting trends in business and science. Born and raised in India, she enrolled in a PhD program in physics in the United States. She soon realized, however, that the future was in information technology, so she switched to a master's program in that field. After working here and there, she and her husband, Subash Lungareddy, decided to return to India to launch their own business. They discussed and studied a number of possibilities, including a unified voice-fax-messaging service and a bandwidth trading site. "We realized it wasn't about the idea," she reflected 10 years later. "The real value is in the execution."[10] So they chose a business for which execution is not just an ingredient for success—it's an absolute must.

They named their baby Ocimum Biosolutions, after the genus of about 25 species of aromatic herbs. Within 10 years of its founding in 2001, the company had become one of the world's premier genomics outsourcing companies. Ocimum is engaged in a wide array of activities, including bio-banking and reference databases, life-science lab information management solutions, bio-IT consulting, and essential research consumables. It serves most of the top 25 global pharmaceutical companies, leading research institutes, and emerging biotech firms. Ancharya is the CEO and a veritable force of nature. In 2006, *Red Herring Magazine* put her on its list of 25 Tech Titans under 35. Two years later, she was named by *Biospectrum* as Entrepreneur of the Year and awarded the prestigious Astia Life Science Innovators Award. And in 2011, the World Economic Forum selected her as one of 190 Young Global Leaders.

Ocimum is based in the so-called Genome Valley in Hyderabad, India, a location that has attracted dozens of domestic and foreign pharmaceutical and biotechnology firms, both large and small. The secret to Ocimum's success owes much to the human and technical resources available in India. But little would become of them without the zeal for rapid growth that has become the distinguishing characteristic of so many emerging market multinationals. Ancharya's style is all about speed and seizing the opportunities for global expansion. She has launched new products, pursued new markets, and made acquisitions at dizzying swiftness, certainly not waiting until her staff was ready to do so. It took her and the small team she assembled in 2001 one year to build Biotracker, a resource planning tool that helps scientists in academic labs manage samples and research processes—"the first product I sold to a customer before it was completely ready, like everyone else does," she conceded with a laugh.[11] (Thanks to this mindset, Ocimum has made it onto the Deloitte ranking of the fastest-growing companies in Asia three years in a row.)

Early in the new century, the company created a gene expression product as well as an innovative RNA software product, iRNA Check, to aid researchers in the silencing of certain genes, the first product of its kind on the market. "At that point, we wanted to build scale," said Ancharya,[12] who had just 25 employees at the time and $1 million in revenue.

And scale she built. In 2004 Ocimum bought the microarray division of MWG, a German client and the leading genomics company in Europe at the time, for $220,000. Microarrays are a series of microscopic DNA spots attached to a solid surface, which are later used to analyze the genes. "Everyone was wondering who was this little company out of India intent on buying a large European company," she remembered. "We received publicity worth around US$1 million."[13] This acquisition gave Ocimum not just valuable technology but also a professional sales team.

In 2006 Ancharya set her eyes on the biomolecules division of Isogen Life Sciences, a Dutch company, which it bought with funding from the International Finance Corporation, the private equity arm of the World Bank. The big step came in 2007 with the acquisition, for $10 million, of the genomic assets division of Gene Logic, a U.S. genomics firm with a market capitalization of $2 billion and an enviable client portfolio that included most large pharmaceutical firms. The firm also had developed unique gene databases.

Like all successful outsourcing companies, Ocimum works closely with clients. The company assigns a team to each client, who spends time with it and then returns to India to explain to the product designers and programmers exactly what is needed. A project typically takes between 3 and 12 months. Like other outsourcers in India, the key advantage at the beginning was cost. Ocimum charges the client $40 per person hour, three or four times less than the typical European or American firm. At those rates, growth and profitability are guaranteed as far as the eye can see.

The future holds many opportunities for a firm like Ocimum. In 2011 and 2012 U.S. pharmaceutical firms saw their patents expire on as many as 10 blockbuster drugs, including Lipitor and Plavix. Also, mergers in the industry mean that cost reductions and other synergies are the new game in town. Biotech companies starved of cash are also turning to outsourcing as a cost-effective strategy. Outsourcing companies stand to win big from these trends. They are repositioning themselves as outsourcing partners, offering clients a complete solution to their genomics needs. Ancharya calls this "Research as a Service"— RaaS. "Earlier biotech companies would get, say, $100 million, and they would spend a lot of money in building a brand new infrastructure, to create a genomics lab," said Ancharya. Now they "realize that you don't really need $3 million for creating a genomics lab [when] you could spend $200,000 in giving this work out to somebody else."[14]

The logic of outsourcing in the life sciences and in pharmaceuticals has become simply irresistible. "We are a global genomics outsourcing company. Essentially what we are trying to do is to provide a combination of software, lab, and mindware to come up with solutions in genomics for what the common pharma and biotech companies are looking for. Whether it is biomarkers, clinical genomics, or anything else in this space, we have a complete solution," said Ancharya. "So, we combine all of that to create an offshore lab."[15] Think of Ocimum as a simultaneous supermarket, convenience store, *and* boutique for global pharmaceutical and biotech companies looking to streamline and rationalize their drug research and development processes.

In less than a decade, Ocimum has come to serve 2,000 customers worldwide from its operational bases in Gaithersburg, Maryland, and Indianapolis in the United States, IJsselstien in the Netherlands, and Hyderabad in India. Speed as strategy and execution as motto have made this company the darling of the global biopharmaceutical industry. The path to global reach, however, is replete with pitfalls, and Ocimum is no exception. In 2011, dwindling orders from U.S. pharmaceutical firms has forced the company to put its American subsidiary up for sale. As

Anu Ancharya says of the rapid growth of her company, "There is a very small border between taking a lot of risk and being stupid."[16] But, of course, without such aggressive risk-taking, Ocimum never could have gotten to where it is today.

Let's see next what lessons we can extract from these experiences with a view to benefiting from speed and avoiding failure.

Global Expansion Is a Sprint, not a Marathon

Emerging market multinationals like BYD, América Móvil, and Ocimum took a different approach to global expansion than the traditional multinationals from Europe and the United States. They and their peers expanded abroad *even before they were ready to do so*. They were willing to accept the inherent risks associated with accelerated expansion because they wanted to be in touch with their customer in as many markets as possible early on in their international expansion and because they understand the importance of learning to be global as quickly as possible. Think of this approach as a hit-*and*-miss template for fast global expansion. In fact, if you do not expand with abandon, you are missing the dynamic captured in Figure 6.

In addition, you may lose once-in-a-lifetime opportunities in foreign countries that require immediate action. In the fast-paced global economy of today, you need to be bold precisely because the upside is so much greater than the downside. If you don't, you have fallen victim to the all-too-human tendency to overestimate losses and underestimate gains. But you need to expand smartly:

- The virtuous circle of international expansion begins with the exposure to new, diverse environments, trends, and requirements. Firms typically engage in a trial-and-error process as they cope with the inevitable failures and

FIGURE 6

The recurrent virtuous circle of rapid global expansion.

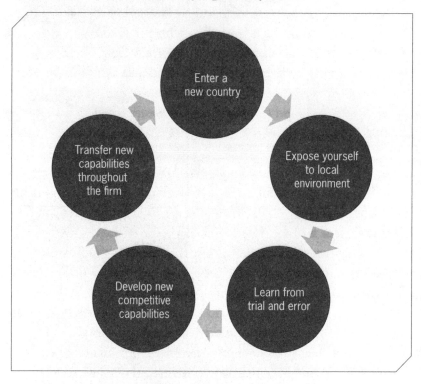

capitalize on the successes. Put another way, they don't get it right through brainstorming in the C-suite; they sweat it out in the trenches. McDonald's stumbled during the late 1960s and 1970s as it tried to replicate its quintessentially American business model in foreign markets. Locating in the Dutch suburbs, for instance, was not the best strategy for selling burgers in countries in which people eat downtown. In truth, of course, there was no way McDonald's could get it right without first being proven wrong. You can anticipate a few things and avoid making some mistakes, but in the world of international business to get where you ultimately want to be, you must be willing to go through the humbling process of discovering your limitations and exposing your company to failure.

- Good management turns the trial-and-error method into a process of organizational learning, teaching managers what does and doesn't work in different contexts and allowing them to share such vital knowledge with the rest of the organization. This is a crucial step in the virtuous circle because learning is always local. In order for the entire company to benefit, it must be shared. BYD's Wang understood this principle from the start, inviting his managers and engineers to interact and share experiences. After all, a good manager is not one who learns and gets ahead but one who enables others to thrive as well.

- Organizational learning, in turn, contributes to the accumulation of new competitive capabilities, which fuel further international expansion into new countries and products, and keep the momentum going. Consider the case of América Móvil. Its dominant position in Latin America gives it scale and bargaining power to negotiate with other telecommunications companies, and with technology and equipment suppliers. In addition, local connections with politicians, regulators, and entrepreneurs established in each new market serve as a basis for identifying and exploiting new business opportunities, even in industries other than telecommunications. Without his company's early and quick expansion, Carlos Slim would not be today the richest man in the world.

- For this recurrent virtuous circle of fast global expansion to work, top managers have to ensure that the new capabilities learned in each country are diffused throughout the firm. A small firm like Ocimum made acquisitions not merely to grow but to learn about new technologies and new markets, with the idea in mind of becoming a full-range genomics outsourcing firm with the ability to serve clients worldwide.

By completing each new cycle of fast expansion the successful global company takes its business model to a new level. Failing to expand rapidly condemns the firm to lag behind bolder players that could well be out of reach by the time your company decides to react. Some trains come your way only once in a lifetime.

No Sacred Cows!

Never fall in love with what brought you success.

Everyone has a plan till they get punched in the mouth.

—MIKE TYSON

IT'S CALLED PATH DEPENDENCY—OR MAYBE JUST BEING stubborn and conceited. Others call it hubris, the worst kind of corporate disease. The better you become at something, the less adept you are at admitting that something's not going right, at reversing course, and responding to competitors. Just like human beings, corporations are creatures of habit. They learn how to do something very well and then forget that perhaps there are other ways and approaches that could enable them to expand or defend their market share and enhance their profitability.

Consider that ingenious nineteenth-century invention the wristwatch. Swiss manufacturers dominated the world market up until the 1950s with their supremely well-crafted mechanical watches—that is, until Timex of the United States came up with an alternative vision for the industry: a cheap, standardized watch powered by a battery. Timex was maybe the most un-Swiss watch ever made, but it sold by the tens of millions. The market was hungry for a timepiece that was affordable and easily available at drugstores and other similar outlets as opposed to jewelries. Moreover, the Swiss watches lasted forever but required periodic cleaning and other repairs, tasks that were expensively performed by the jewelers. Timex watches didn't promise to last a lifetime, but as the company boasted in advertisements, its watches could "take a licking and keep on ticking" and didn't require frequent repairs. What's more, they were so inexpensive that when one went bad, you could simply dispose of it and buy a new one. The Swiss companies didn't think they should be in the business of making cheap watches for the masses. They were too proud to do that—and too concerned about tarnishing their image —and thus they missed the boat completely.

Before the Swiss or even Timex had time to react, another American firm, Bulova, designed a watch whose time mechanism was a so-called tuning fork, a bifurcated piece of metal. When struck, it vibrates with a steady frequency that can be used to measure time. The technology had been invented in Switzerland, but again, no Swiss firm was ready to abandon the centuries-old practice of making watches with lots of tiny gears and springs— after all, they still reigned supreme in the luxury segment of the market. Bulova watches contained fewer components and were cheaper to make, lasted longer without repair, and were more accurate. They took the market by storm while the Swiss once more stood on shore, watching profits sail away.

The Swiss also invented the quartz watch, but neither they nor the American firms took advantage of the innovation. Two Japanese firms, Seiko and Citizen, made hefty profits by mass-producing quartz timepieces. Quartz is a natural crystal that vibrates when an electric current is run through it. They are even cheaper to make and more accurate than those using tuning-fork technology. True, during the 1960s, the two Japanese firms had to fight the perception in the market that quartz watches were inferior to American, let alone Swiss, watches, but the marketplace eventually adjusted and the American firms never recovered from the flood of Japanese-made quartz watch exports.

Meanwhile, back in Switzerland, massive losses and layoffs shook the national conscience. Watchmaking was as much part of the Swiss psyche as Gruyère cheese, and precisely for that reason, it took a complete outsider by the name of Nicolas Hayek to turn things around. After launching the Swatch in the early 1980s, Hayek single-handedly reclaimed the lion's share of the global watch market for his adopted country of Switzerland. Not only was Hayek foreign born—he hailed from Lebanon—he'd gained his industry expertise in a completely different field: automobiles.

Underwhelmed by the sacred cows of watchmaking, Hayek challenged the conventional wisdom and redefined each of the detailed tasks involved in the business, from design and manufacturing to marketing and sales. His experience as a consultant to the automobile industry gave him the idea of reducing the number of components down to 51 from nearly 130, thus enhancing the possibilities for automating the manufacturing process, a crucial step to take in a high-wage country such as Switzerland.

The Swiss comeback in watchmaking is more the exception than the rule, and the match is not yet over. Just as upstart American firms once challenged the two Swiss watchmaking cartels, so now Indian and Chinese firms are starting to challenge Swatch's global dominance. The more confident the Swiss are that their watch is unassailable, the better the chances their competitive edge will disappear in a relative heartbeat.

In fact, the list of established companies in the United States, Europe, and Japan that have fallen into the competency trap of thinking they were invincible is long and growing. Let's use initials here to protect corporate identities: NCR, ABB, ICI, AEG, NEC, JAL, and on and on. If these names were carved on tombstones, they would make for an impressive corporate graveyard. Blind adherence to what worked in the past undid all these erstwhile corporate giants, widely regarded once upon a time as examples to emulate. Meanwhile, emerging market multinationals are thinking outside the box and charging right past established companies all across the developed world.

Finding New Ways of Competing

We have already seen many illustrations of the new rules of competition pioneered by emerging market multinationals. In bread making, Bimbo surged past Sara Lee by executing before strategizing and by focusing on executing after a workable strategy was put in place. Embraer followed the same pathway in regional jets in order to surpass Bombardier. In the fast-moving world of IT services, Infosys irrupted onto the global stage by following the same formula: *execute, strategize, then execute again.*

The management lesson here is not that emerging market multinationals will always win or that they are inherently superior at executing efficiently, effectively, and on time. The more important point is that superior execution can be learned and can become the basis for adapting the company's strategy in real time or even for reinventing the company. After all, that's exactly what IBM achieved when it got out of the computer business.

Or consider the Coca-Cola Company. It made and sold carbonated brown sugar water for decades, turning itself into a veritable machine for printing money. Shareholders and top management made fortunes—back in the early 1990s Roberto Goizueta was the first CEO to break the billion-dollar barrier in annual compensation. Everything was going according to plan, until consumers changed their mind and shifted their preferences toward water, juice, and sports drinks. The guys in Atlanta couldn't understand what was going on. They insisted that Coca-Cola was a soft-drink company, straight and simple. The company ground up four CEOs over the course of a single decade before realizing that it was in the *beverage* business. Making Coca-Cola innovate required going back to the drawing board. Executives had to do market research, come up with new brands, position them in the right segment, and think through all the details about procurement, bottling, distribution, and sale—a gargantuan task for a firm long used to telling the consumer what to drink, and still it wasn't an entirely successful undertaking. While Coca-Cola is roaring in key markets like Japan or Mexico, it still trails Pepsi in China and is badly behind in bottled water and sports drinks worldwide, although it has managed to turn the tide in juices and canned coffee.

The moral: Coca-Cola's addiction to carbonated drinks almost brought the company down. You can't let your star product become a sacred cow. Being highly successful and profitable with something can blind you to new trends in the market and render you unwilling to abandon strategies and products that are no longer tenable. A company locked into the self-complacency of past success sooner or later is going to the canvas, just like a boxer who is badly prepared for a fight. It's a state of mind that needs to be avoided at all costs.

As the Coca-Cola case demonstrates, reinventing the corporation to meet new demands or circumstances is no easy task. Internal and external resistance must be overcome. Individuals and companies are subject to inertia. We tend to escalate our commitment to a course of action we believe effective and successful even after receiving disconfirming feedback. It's a perfectly human tendency and flaw. We hope that things will turn around and that circumstances will return to a state we consider as normal, one that does not require adaptation or doing away with the sacred cows. Managers can easily fool themselves into thinking that nothing of significance is changing. Employees and suppliers, too, are likely to reinforce the feeling of calm just before the storm. They may be too averse to change for the good of the company, convinced that the old sacred ways will eventually prove as useful and effective as in the good old days.

Certainly, your competitors will do nothing to encourage you to change either, especially the emerging market multinationals. While you enjoy the fleeting profits generated by the old way of doing things, they will keep on improving their products and their operations. Acer, Samsung, and BYD were sitting by the sidelines, watching their industries evolve and preparing themselves for the big assault on the established companies. They imagined a better way of competing, and they took everyone by surprise when they catapulted themselves to leading positions in the global market.

Seeing the Opportunity in the Hidden Corners of the Market

Consider next the idea that niches can become stepping-stones into the mainstream of the market. Proud and stubborn firms like Electrolux, Whirlpool, and GE saw Haier coming into their backyard. They could see that the Chinese upstart was emphasizing small segments of the market that they did not care about, but they dismissed Haier as a marginal player from a developing country. Big mistake.

Heineken lost its prized distinction as the world's leading import beer to Modelo's Corona, which managed the niche with more conviction and passion. L'Oréal's reluctance to use direct sales channels led the firm to lose important opportunities in emerging economies, paving the way for firms such as Natura to succeed and facilitating also the expansion of established firms like Avon, with more experience in direct sales. "Cater to the niches" is the twenty-first-century response to the twentieth-century obsession with the mainstream of the mass market.

To be successful, niche thinking needs to permeate the entire corporate culture. For many years, BMW seemed incapable of doing anything wrong. It reigned supreme in the segment of sporty sedans, one that no other company managed to occupy. The "machine for driving" was simply invincible—until the Bavarian firm lost its focus in an attempt to expand its presence into the mainstream of the market without a good plan. In 1994 it acquired Rover, the troubled British automaker, and couldn't make it compete. "We set out targets," one senior BMW executive admitted, "but left them to get on with it."[1] After a mere six years, BMW dished Rover to a group of British investors, the so-called Phoenix Consortium, who couldn't make any good of it either. The company was later liquidated, with Chinese SAIC Motor Corporation Limited acquiring part of its assets. After admitting its mistake and rectifying, BMW is blooming again by sticking to its winning formula: German engineering for the discerning auto owner who loves to feel the road.

Apple also seemed to have lost its way in the 1990s. Observers declared the company dead in the wake of the computer-clone revolution. Instead of taking the established companies head on, Apple went back to its roots, designing computers that were easy to use, cute, and full of personality. The plan was to appeal not only to the minds but also to the hearts and senses of its buyers, turning them into unconditional fans. Apple succeeded where most other companies tend to fail, by transforming a commodity product into an object of desire. It takes conviction and resolution to swim against the stream, to reject the conventional wisdom, to choose a course opposite to the one taken by your competitors.

Today BMW and Apple are among the world's most valuable brands, but they were in no way entitled to success. In fact, managers almost killed the brand by drifting away from their winning formula. Some products and some brands are simply made for a niche. If you want to go mainstream, then you need to come up with a different formula. That's what Swatch did. It did not seek to reposition Omega or Longines outside the natural and logical segment for those upscale brands. Rather, it launched a new brand, mass-producing colorful watches for customers seeking a youthful style in a Swiss watch.

Preempting the Competition

One of the most devastating examples of path dependency and falling prey to sacred cows is the way in which many established firms from Europe, Japan, and the United States forgot that scale can be everything, especially when it comes to shocking your competitors by preempting them. This is a prime area in which emerging market multinationals have beaten the market leaders of the past at their own game. Samsung conquered the global consumer electronics market by making bold bets on ever-larger manufacturing plants to make innovative products using the newest technologies. The likes of Sony, Panasonic, and Philips simply didn't dare to match the South Korean firm. Kraft lost its leadership in candy for the same reason, stalling on its own caution while the bold Argentine firm, Arcor, took over top global status. In the world of wind turbines, companies such as Sinovel or Suzlon are rapidly gaining ground relative to powerhouses like GE Wind following the same principle of scaling to win.

Anheuser-Busch, even before its merger with Brazil's InBev, understood the importance of scale in production and distribution. It chose to blanket the market with brands and ramp up volumes fast. It makes billions of dollars in profits by selling a zillion servings each year. True, thousands of boutique brewers do just fine without becoming huge. But notice that even Modelo of Mexico needed to sell large volumes of its niche-oriented Corona brand in order to turn a profit. And let's not forget that beer is not a functional product meant to satisfy some physical need.

Beer is characterized by social and sensory attributes: you don't drink beer alone, you enjoy it with your friends after a day at the office or while watching sports. The brand almost conveys a lifestyle, a way of having fun. The bigger the scale, the bigger the party. Successful scaling frequently means worrying about how the customer will perceive the product, not just making lots of it.

Scaling is not necessarily at odds with preserving a taste for the unique and the well crafted. Brands like Swatch or Zara sell by the millions but have managed to retain a sense of exclusivity. They shape customer expectations by launching collections and creating a sense of scarcity. While it is true that watches and clothes lend themselves to this type of market positioning, not all companies get it right. In fact, most get it awfully wrong. Seiko and Casio both lost their ability to capture the imagination of watch buyers. Or think about how the Gap managed its way to decline by ignoring the simple truth that people seek style and differentiation when it comes to clothes.

A telling example of the importance of scaling that has little to do with fashion is Huawei's rise to the top of the global telecommunications equipment industry, a business once dominated by the likes of Siemens, Cisco, and Alcatel. The firm saw an opening in the market by catering to the unique needs of rapidly growing operators such as Telefónica, América Móvil, and the large Chinese firms. Huawei did not compromise on quality, customization, or service. The company fought hard to win customers specifically so it could build rapidly up scale.

Thriving on Chaos

Nowhere is the increasing competitive edge enjoyed by emerging market multinationals more clearly felt than when it comes to taking advantage of one of the key characteristics of the new global economy of the twenty-first century: chaos. Acer of Taiwan did not outpace IBM, Dell, and HP because it had superior technology. It prevailed over them because of its homegrown ability to cope with uncertainty, ambiguity, and complexity. It learned how to navigate the turbulent waters of the industry and the global economy, and then deployed that expertise throughout its worldwide operations. Acer accepted risk as constant in the new competitive landscape and turned it into an advantage.

Orascom Telecom of Egypt has succeeded in the same way, expanding into some of the most inhospitable markets in the world, places like Iraq and North Korea. Bharat Forge managed to become the world's second-largest forging company by overcoming the shortcomings of the chaotic business setting in India. The new global economy demands that companies cope with chaos not by avoiding it but by turning it into a distinct capability, by embracing it. This is another sacred cow to avoid: the idea that risk is something to be afraid of.

Look at how American banks rushed out of Latin America in the wake of the infamous debt crisis of 1982. One government after another defaulted on its bonds, throwing the entire financial sector into disarray. The likes of Citibank, Bank of Boston, and Bank of America were scathed and scared, and vowed never ever again to make the same mistake. While the region went through a decade of sluggish economic growth and hyperinflation, it eventually recovered, presenting a golden opportunity for banks that dared seize it.

Anticipating the upswing, Canadian and, especially, Spanish banks took advantage of a wide-open opportunity. They acquired Latin American banks by the dozens. They sent expats to clean up the balance sheets, establish risk assessment procedures, and set up state-of-the-art information systems. Then they moved from one country to the next, creating a truly regional banking franchise. Instead of catering to the relatively safe upper segment of the well off, they targeted the masses, encouraging them to deposit at the bank the money they hoarded under the mattress. It was a risky bet. But by embracing chaos, Santander and BBVA established themselves as the largest banks in the region by the start of the new century. Today, they are laughing all the way to the bank—their own—watching Latin American economies grow and prosper. In 2011, Santander made more than half of its $5 billion in annual profits in Latin America. Yes, *$5 billion.*[2]

Or think about the Brazilian, Indian, and Chinese mining firms that are investing in sub-Saharan Africa like there's no tomorrow. Africa is at the high point of the so-called long arc of geopolitical instability that stretches from Latin America all the way to Southeast Asia, and includes such chronically unstable regions as the Caucasus and the Middle East as well. Market-oriented reform governments, often corrupt, dot this part of the world that is so well endowed with natural resources. Operating successfully as a mining company is not as simple as going in, paying bribes, and getting out. You won't succeed if you follow that model—and you will place your company in legal jeopardy. You need to be smart about uncertainty, political turmoil, and chaos. In addition to the government, you have to deal with opposition groups, environmentalists, human-rights activists, community leaders, and competitors. You can't ignore the full range of stakeholders. You must engage them.

Vale of Brazil, the world's third-largest mining company, shows how to do it. Vale has a presence in Angola, Mozambique, the Democratic Republic of Congo, Guinea, and South Africa. Like other smart mining companies, it invests heavily not only in plant and equipment but also in relationships, nurturing ties all across the board to create a base of support for its activities. This is exactly how you embrace chaos in order to thrive on it. Research indicates that mining companies that invest relatively small amounts of resources and managerial time in cultivating stakeholder relations reap billions of dollars in increased market capitalization.

But political instability is just one dimension of chaos. There are also the difficulties of doing business under conditions of infrastructure and resource deficits. From their birth, many emerging market multinationals have had to do more with less, proving time and again that necessity is the mother of invention and sometimes launching innovations that change industry rules. Take the case of Zhongxing Medical. This Chinese company developed an X-ray device that generates direct digital images costing just 10 percent of the cost of equivalent devices made by established multinationals.

The bad news for old-line firms: companies used to operating in chaotic environments can drive you out of the industry. The good news: you can set up R&D units in those countries to innovate on the cheap. GE Healthcare has used its R&D centers in emerging economies to develop local-market products that later were adopted worldwide, like its famous handheld electrocardiogram device.

Switching Course through Acquisitions

The path to global riches has frequently entailed being on the watch for corporate acquisitions. Emerging market multinationals have the cash to acquire their way to the top thanks both to the profits generated in their rapidly expanding domestic markets and to their export competitiveness. But all companies would be wise to learn from them the principle of acquiring smart, of buying what makes sense strategically and only if it brings to the company something that can be useful once integrated with existing operations. Tenaris of Argentina became the leading supplier of tubular goods to the oil industry by thinking about its business as one requiring a worldwide network of integrated facilities offering a service to its customers as seamlessly global as the products it makes. Cemex also acquired smartly and integrated cement factories and distribution systems around the world in order to gain an edge over famed competitors like Holcim. Tata Communications, a newcomer to the world of global voice telecommunications, turned its Indian origins and membership in the Tata group of companies to its advantage, succeeding where giants BellSouth and AT&T had failed. Tata's secret: thinking big and building, piece by piece, a global presence to cater to the needs of global customers.

Smart acquisitions enabled Tenaris, Cemex, and Tata Communications to win big in ways that their competitors could not because they were hostage to the old thinking that acquisitions are trophies to be displayed as proof of their success. In fact, acquisitions are only the first step on the long way to success. For years, GM and Ford displayed their acquisitions as if they were works of art. Neither could be bothered to learn much from Saab and Volvo, the storied Swedish automobile brands that they acquired in 1990 and 1999, respectively. Sure, GM and Ford managers were thrilled because they could request a Saab or a Volvo as the company car, but they did little to make the acquisitions work and even less to see how they could enhance the competitiveness of the parent company. Rather, they treated the newcomers as silos separate from the rest of the corporation, thus foregoing any possibility of cross-fertilization.

The Detroit approach to acquisitions is a far cry from the hands-on way in which Unilever handles the process. The Anglo-Dutch food group likes to write multibillion-dollar checks. Who doesn't? Consider ice cream, where Unilever is the largest global player, with an 18 percent market share. In order to get there, they digested Popsicle, Klondike, Mio, Breyers, Kibon, Ben & Jerry's, and dozens of other ice-cream brands worldwide. So did Nestlé, its archrival, which acquired Clarke Foods, Dairymaid, Dreyer's, Dairy World, Schöller, and bits and pieces of Häagen-Dazs to reach nearly 13 percent global market share. But Unilever stays ahead of the game by constantly reorganizing its portfolio of brands, looking for synergies in production and distribution, and exploiting niches in the market through savvy marketing and advertising. No emerging market multinational has yet challenged Unilever's dominant position, in large part because when it comes to sacred cows, Unilever thinks as if it were an emerging market firm still struggling up from its roots: it never stays still, never takes anything for granted, is never complacent about its accomplishments, and never hesitates to change in response to new threats and opportunities.

Be Cautious, at Your Own Risk

Faced with the complexity, risks, and pitfalls of the global economy of the twenty-first century, many companies become paralyzed by the notion that cautious expansion into other markets is the best recipe for success. Not so the emerging market multinationals. BYD, the Chinese battery maker, has a good chance of becoming the world's leading electric vehicle maker thanks to its daring plans for global expansion. América Móvil has succeeded where BellSouth once failed, following the same principle of expanding with abandon. Its dominance in the Latin American mobile telecommunications market is testament to the principle that it is never too early to think about foreign markets. Fact is, if you wait until you're ready, you've waited too long. In pioneering the offshore lab, Ocimum Biosolutions has challenged companies in its industry and beyond by exploiting the intersection between IT and the life sciences, moving aggressively to build a global presence, and never wasting time looking back at the road traveled.

McDonald's is a good example of an established firm that was once obsessed by being cautious but managed to become bolder over time. The fast-food chain was the most methodical and risk-averse company in the world. It had a globally recognized brand desired by billions but preferred not to venture into sketchy countries. Why bother with the risky parts of the world if you can make money comfortably in the United States and a handful of safe markets such as Japan, Britain, and France? In fact, the company didn't enter a market one might consider politically problematic or chaotic until it turned 50 years old.

Once it had saturated safe markets with too many restaurants, however, McDonald's had no other choice but to embrace chaos—and it did. Eastern Europe, China, Africa, the Middle East, and South Asia all became home to the Golden Arches. McDonald's had to create supply networks from scratch, deal with governments that evicted it from prime retail locations (such as the famous one off Tiananmen Square), and train employees that had little understanding for the means and ways of its vintage smiley service. The company relied on local partners in many of these risky markets in order to learn the ropes. It trained managers to cope with the unexpected and prepared itself to deal with chaos on a grand scale.

Nothing Is Sacrosanct

In previous chapters we've learned the new rules of global competition written by the emerging market multinationals. We've also seen that they have no monopoly over these rules—these are principles that can be adopted and learned. Sadly, though, very few companies from the developed countries are listening and willing to change their ways. Many believe that things will turn around in some magical way. Others are trying to adapt but find themselves stuck in old thought patterns. If the competency trap were inevitable and impossible to escape, there would be little point to mentioning it here: emerging market multinationals win, old-line global behemoths lose—game over, case closed.

But being able to redefine the established business model is not the sole province of the new multinationals.

In electronics, for instance, Philips took a clear-eyed look at emerging market competition and chose a different path than most of its developed-world counterparts, the likes of Sweden's Electrolux and Japan's Panasonic. Executives began by acknowledging that the company's existing operations were beyond repair, then spared no sacred cows in meeting the challenge: they jettisoned plants, workers, entire divisions, and old organizational practices. Company leaders decided to outsource all production of such commodity products and components as bulbs, CRTs, monitors, speakers, chips, TVs, VCRs, and DVDs, while retaining control over brand and distribution channels. Then they poured resources into lighting systems and health-care solutions, researching and designing new technologies that bundle hardware, software, and services to win over customers worldwide. Today, while Philips makes billions in annual profits, Panasonic and Sony are losing both market share and money.

Volkswagen provides an equally powerful illustration of how enlightened corporate leadership can meet the competitive challenge posed by the emerging market multinationals. Like Philips, Volkswagen went through years of financial underperformance and painful layoffs before realizing that meeting the new competitive dynamics of the industry meant getting rid of sacred cows. The company now makes automobiles all over the world, using German technology to be sure, but taking advantage of a globally integrated approach to product design, manufacturing, and marketing. While Hyundai, Tata Motors, and Geely may one day pose an even more formidable challenge than the Japanese did, Volkswagen has demonstrated a flexibility and versatility that will be difficult to match.

Another company that adapted to changing circumstances is chemical giant DuPont. The company grew during the twentieth century by exploiting the inventions generated by its R&D department, including nylon, neoprene, and Teflon. But in the new century, this long-successful business model of inventing, producing, and selling generic materials ran headlong into high market turbulence and increased competition. So DuPont Chairman and CEO Ellen Kullman decided to shift direction by making the company more customer oriented. Today, DuPont defines itself as a "market-driven science company" and "Global Collaboratory" more focused on its activities and engaged in collaboration projects with clients in order to provide them with the materials and solutions they need to manufacture better products.

The key takeaway: nothing has been inexorable about the rise of the emerging market multinationals. They have embraced the seven principles contained in this book, something that companies from other countries can emulate. If IBM, Philips, DuPont, and Volkswagen could do it, so can your company. The key is to revisit every sacred principle, every object of adoration that has become part of your company's legend.

Finding the Hidden Treasure

In the multipolar world of the twenty-first century, corporate leaders must pay attention to mundane details and challenge their organization to constantly revisit old ways of thinking and doing. They must follow the winding path in Figure 7 to find their company's place under the sun of the new global economy.

Start your voyage of discovery by executing well before you come up with, and commit to, a grand strategy. And then don't forget about sustaining execution. Identify neglected niches that offer wide avenues for success, and then scale your operations to win. Embrace chaos, acquire smart, and expand with abandon

FIGURE 7

A treasure map for competing in the new global economy.

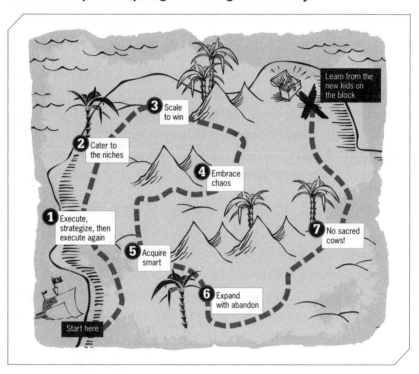

in order to surpass your competitors. A permanent revolution is what's needed—no sacred cows! And don't forget to learn from the new kids on the block. They came from the emerging economies, they are masters at making the most out of scarce resources, they are street smart, they're eager to make it to the top, and they're here to stay.

Take Action!

*Learn how to emulate the success of
the emerging market multinationals.*

Action is the antidote to despair.

—JOAN BAEZ

IN THIS BOOK WE HAVE WALKED YOU THROUGH THE MANY successes of the emerging market multinationals. We have sung their praises because of an uncanny combination of prudence and boldness, their attention to the global and the local, and their ability to surmount the most formidable challenges with relatively scant resources. Emerging market multinationals have come to dominate global industries such as bread, candy, household appliances, consumer electronics, personal computers, wind power, telecommunications, even regional aircraft, with many more poised to make it into the big leagues of global business over the next few years. Brazil's JBC is already the world's largest meat company. Another Brazilian firm, TAM, is about to merge with Chile's LAN to create the world's largest airline by market capitalization. DP World of Dubai is the fourth-largest port operator, and Russia's Gazprom the largest energy group (excluding oil companies). If your industry has not yet been affected by competition from the emerging economies, get ready. It won't be long before you have to compete with them head-to-head.

In the previous chapters, we laid out the big lessons that emerging market multinationals have to teach: how executing before strategizing, catering to the niches, scaling to win, embracing chaos, acquiring smart, and expanding with abandon can pave your way to global excellence. We also implored you to avoid sacred cows, those habits of the mind and of the heart that can lead you astray. In this concluding chapter, we move on to exactly how you and your company can benefit from the principles that have made the emerging market multinationals so competitive and admirable.

Executing before Strategizing

Lesson One: Executing must take precedence over strategizing, although both are needed to succeed. Successful strategies do not come out of the blue. They have to provide a sound value proposition for the customer, and your company should be second to none in putting this into practice. Here are some steps to implement this axiom at your organization:

- Don't waste time thinking through your strategy to the smallest detail. Get feedback from the market quickly and don't be afraid of experimenting, taking chances, and doing whatever is needed to improve your value proposition. Research indicates that most great leaders and most great companies are the result of this messy process of real-time strategy. They adapt and upgrade strategy on the fly. The truth is, you rarely hit upon a great business idea just by thinking about it. Huawei, the Chinese telecommunications equipment giant, rose to prominence not through endless planning but by painstakingly improving its operational execution and attention to detail.

- As you muddle through, start thinking about the implications of what you're doing and how well (or poorly) your company is adding value to the customer. Learn from both successes and failures. Constantly update your priors. Look for the emergent strategy in what you do and how you do it. Embraer has been on the brink of bankruptcy several times only to reemerge as the global regional jet leader. Perhaps it's in the nature of the industry, but this Brazilian firm has made an art and a science of learning from its mistakes. Or consider Hyundai's daring drive to gain market share in the United States and Europe with its relatively affordable and increasingly reliable automobiles.

- Once you have identified the strategy that works, convey it to your colleagues, your bosses, your subordinates, and the entire organization. And by all means sustain your level of excellence at execution. Even the best strategy can run the ship ashore if it's executed haphazardly. Acer had a brilliant idea for the U.S. market back in the 1990s—an Internet-enabled computer, the Aspire—but it launched Aspire without having developed the companion expertise to crack the world's most competitive market.

- Don't hesitate to challenge established practices and ways of doing things inside your company. Take advantage of any opportunity to improve your execution capabilities. When incorporating IT into the company, moving operations overseas, redesigning your structure or outsourcing activities, try to redefine all of your processes to improve your efficiency and time to market. Remember the Cemex Way and how it enabled this company to outperform competitors in cost and quality.

- Do not try to do everything by yourself. The world is full of opportunities to learn. Improve your execution by studying what others are doing elsewhere. Look around to discover who is developing new best practices and try to incorporate them within your business model. As a slow innovator, Matsushita of Japan (now Panasonic) recently decided to ally itself with Samsung, Toshiba, and Olympus to launch new consumer electronics products.
- We're encouraging you to think about the rise of the emerging market multinationals as something akin to a mental revolution—a new way of viewing the forces that shape global competition. We have been taught that big success requires thinking big and acting big. Companies such as Bimbo in bread or Embraer in regional aircraft, by contrast, took small steps that accumulated into something very big. They paid attention to detail and looked beyond the low-hanging fruit to find new ways of competing. The managers at these firms weren't thinking in terms of a big bang in the short run. Their bosses and the owners of the firm didn't ask them to do so, and they took it to heart. They kept themselves busy with the tiniest details but without losing track of the overall picture. Keep in mind the answer given by a thirteenth-century mason when a pilgrim asked why he was carving a piece of stone. He was building a cathedral, the mason explained, even though the structure would not be completed until three centuries later.

It is often said that we learn by doing. That's exactly what focusing on execution is all about. If you don't come up with the strategy, the method, or the product yourself, you are reinventing somebody else's wheel, we've been told. Well, it turns out that following other people's footprints can lead you to striking discoveries or to new ways of competing. Pundits like to talk about taking the road less traveled—what some call the blue ocean—but emerging market multinationals have succeeded in many cases by treading waters populated by established companies. They learned from them, emulating their successes and exploiting their failures. Avoiding your competitors or staying away from them is not necessarily the way to win in the networked global economy of the twenty-first century. You can also engage them, emulate them, and improve upon what they do.

You're striking the right balance between executing and strategizing if you are gaining ground on competitors even before formulating, let alone implementing, a winning strategy.

Catering to the Niches

We have also insisted that market niches are opportunities, windows, and sometimes shortcuts to success when expanding abroad. The essence of our message is that it is really hard to fight against established leaders in an open battlefield and with their same weapons. If you find yourself in that situation, it is much better to adopt guerrilla tactics and look for underserved market segments in which customers demand products or services specifically suited to their needs. At the end of the day, these segments could be a solid basis for further expansion, once you've got a foothold in a foreign country. Capitalizing on niches requires a number of ingredients:

- First, you have to identify and exploit the attributes of your products that make them different from those of the established multinationals. If you have these attributes already developed, half the work is done. The other half is to find the niche markets wherever they might be in the world. Remember the case of Natura Cosméticos—perhaps the only company in the world that can claim to have natural components from the Amazonian rain forest supplied to its factories while *always* meeting the most demanding standards of sustainability and social responsibility.

- Another excellent platform for exploiting niches abroad is having the uncanny ability to adapt your products to the specific needs of specific groups of customers. In that case, you have to find the niche and then make the adaptation work. That means reading widely, talking to people outside your circle of close friends, and carefully observing what is going on. The global economy of the twenty-first century is rich in demographic, economic, social, political, and cultural change. Hidden in that confusing mix of trends are profitable niches for you to exploit. Think about the students targeted by Haier with its fridges or the freezer with a pullout drawer developed by following a customer suggestion.

- Be disciplined. If you want to pursue a niche you've identified as potentially profitable, you must devote your heart and mind to it—and keep your eye on the ball. What were the odds that Embraer could succeed with aircraft assembled in an emerging country? However, its tenacity in exploiting market opportunities in the regional aircrafts segment was the key to becoming a global player in an industry that always belonged to the developed world.

- Bottom line: there are two, not just one, viable niche strategies. The first is to be a global niche player, targeting the same customer profile with the same product or service worldwide. The second is to be a discriminator, catering to different niches in different national markets. In both cases, you need to think beyond the niche after you have dominated it to exploit opportunities in the mainstream of the market. Like the great chess masters, always try to be multiple moves ahead of the action on the board.

Niches should be thought of as a Trojan horse. That's the way in which Haier took the American household appliance market: first by stealth, then by storm. Incorporating what makes you different in your value proposition and delivering it to specific niches is an easy way to gain a foothold in foreign markets. That is how successful emerging market multinationals have paved their way to global leadership: by looking for customers who value what they do differently. Don't make the mistake of thinking that customers and markets are homogeneous around the world. They are not. Not all customers prefer standardization and global brands. In fact, this is good news for companies that are different. Look at Corona and Natura Cosméticos. They benefited from attributes related to their home country: a beer positioned as a tropical, exotic product, and rain forest active ingredients that are extremely difficult to replicate by established multinationals. You don't necessarily have to play the country-of-origin card, however. You only have to deliver something really different than the mainstream product or service. In the end, standardization never makes everybody happy. There's profit in customers ready to rebel against the tyranny of the mainstream. Make them your next niche.

Figure out what you do best that your competitors are not also supplying. Find a growing market with a need for your specific capability. Plot the point on the horizon where these two potentials converge.

Scaling to Win

You can't even hope to win in the global economy of the twenty-first century unless you come to terms with scale. The world market has become a big place. It's no longer the few hundred million people in Europe and the United States that count. Over three billion people in emerging economies have now become eager consumers. Even if you decide to focus all of your attention on a well-defined niche, the global market is still overwhelmingly big. Attractive markets these days run into the billions of dollars. You shouldn't settle for anything less than that.

There's an art and a science to betting on a large market, though. You can't just invest and wish for the best. That's a recipe for disaster as companies from both developed and emerging economies have found. Ask South Korea's Daewoo or Italy's Benetton. They overinvested in manufacturing and distribution capacity without having a plan as to how to sell their automobiles and sweaters. Here's what you should do:

- Identify the shortest and smoothest path to scale. You can achieve scale in multiple ways: by increasing the number of national markets you enter or by expanding your product offerings, or both. Don't be dogmatic about it. Choose the path that suits your company and the circumstances. Hyundai is doing well nowadays because it fiercely expanded its global reach, taking losses at first to succeed later.
- Link the process of building up the scale of your operations to the process of learning. You should scale up only in areas where you feel confident you have the knowledge, the capabilities, and the resources to win. You don't have to grow across the board. Swatch, the global leader in wristwatches, decided to increase its manufacturing of watch movements to a much greater extent than finished watches. It sold its excess production to its competitors in Asia, which became dependent on the Swiss giant for the most critical component in the final product.
- Never think about scale as a goal in itself. It's a process, a way for your company to become a better competitor. You build up scale in order to meet the needs of your customers around the world, to attract the best suppliers, and to preempt competitors from invading your turf.

- Don't let scale tarnish your company's reputation for design, quality, or the ability to customize. The more customers you have, the easier it should be for you to make better products with more variations. We are no longer living in the days of Henry Ford, when every product had to be the same. Look at Tata Motors. It is building up a portfolio of brands without abandoning scale. In a few years, it will be ready to take on the world.
- Don't hesitate to team up with other companies to build scale if you need to. Benetton in the United States or Häagen-Dazs in Europe decided to go it alone without having the capabilities and the resources to do so. They entered foreign markets building a huge production and distribution infrastructure without thinking about how they could attract enough customers. They could have won big had they acknowledged their limitations and sought to overcome them with the help of other companies.

Many companies invest big because they see no other way of competing. They feel that unless they can spread their large fixed costs over a big customer base, they will be driven out of the market. Before committing to scale, try instead to think through how you can become a leaner and more capable company. Identify the pockets of excellence embedded in your organization. Make sure that you are not trying to conceal your weaknesses by engaging in an investment spree. If you can't overcome your limitations, try to play to your strengths. No company is excellent across the board, not even Apple, which is great at perfecting products and creating eco-systems around them (all of those app designers) but awful at inventing new technologies. The trick is not always to come up with something radically new, but to make existing products and technologies more functional, easier to use, and more attractive to the customer—in a word, *cooler.* Or take the example of Philips. As we saw in the last chapter, the Dutch firm limped along for two decades before recognizing that it couldn't compete by being a mass producer of cheap consumer electronics—the Japanese, the Koreans, and now the Chinese are much better at that game. Finally, Phillips outsourced manufacturing and focused on what it could do well: research and development, selling, and servicing sophisticated lighting and medical systems.

We often hear that size matters, and the reality is that it does—in more ways than one. We are convinced that no great company should remain small. But many companies undermine their own status, credibility, and profitability by scaling in the wrong way. Don't do what Siemens did: lose millions in the cellphone industry by overexpanding. Look instead at Samsung, Arcor, and Suzlon, the three emerging market multinationals that we proposed as prime examples of scaling to win. They first developed the capabilities to scale by paying attention to execution. Or look at Haier, the company that started by focusing on a niche and then built scale as it extended its product line. The little secret about scaling to win is that you need to know when to do it. Not every company is ready to grow big at the same time in the evolutionary process.

Is your company's scale growing faster than the market? That's the metric that counts.

Embracing Chaos

We live in a complicated world. The sooner you understand that, the sooner you'll be prepared to conquer it. And the best way to be prepared is to be immersed in the complications associated with emerging economies: subpar infrastructure, red tape, political instability, underdeveloped financial markets, and on and on. It is called the advantage of the underdog—what doesn't kill you makes you stronger. If you are used to these environments, it's easy for you to get the knack of how to thrive in them. Think of the telecommunications industry. When growth opportunities in the developed world are already exploited, the future lies in emerging countries, and this clearly favors the rise of emerging market multinationals. Remember that Orascom Telecom did not blink at entering Algeria despite the chaotic political environment because things in Egypt were not much different.

But that said, all the advantage doesn't necessarily lie with emerging market multinationals when it comes to coping with chaotic business environments. Dealing with chaos is all about finding innovative ways to overcome these complexities, and whatever your country of origin, that requires clear thinking more than anything else. Here are some tips for starting to see the glass half full:

- Don't throw in the towel because you lack the resources or budget of bigger competitors. Some of the most important innovations in the world came from people who questioned the conventional wisdom and proved possible what others had dismissed. For instance, Tata has proved to the world that products such as cars or water purifiers can be completely redesigned to be sold at only a fraction of the price of the products of traditional multinationals, as the examples of the Tata Nano car or the Tata Swach water purifier show. Thinking this way will help you to overcome any lack of resources. In short, don't take anything for granted. Question everything.
- Network-like structures can help overcome chaos and the lack of resources, especially when you build organizational systems that enable the company and its partners to define a win-win relationship. That is how Chinese motorbike assemblers such as Longxin and Zongshen have pushed the outsourcing of components to the limit by dividing the final product into modules and imposing

on their subcontractors rough parameters such as weight and size. Longxin is now the main Chinese exporter of motorbikes.

- These partnerships can also be used when expanding abroad, as Acer did to overcome its lack of financial resources. By doing so, the company found an excellent balance between global coordination and local responsiveness.

- In chaotic environments, stakeholders such as politicians and regulators have more power than in developed countries. Think of this power as an opportunity. Put yourself in the shoes of politicians and regulators when dealing with them, and again try always to define win-win scenarios as Orascom did when entering North Korea. In exchange for investments and services that pushed the development of the country forward, Orascom gained excellent entry conditions.

- Never be naïve, however, when dealing with foreign governments, especially in environments where you are overexposed to the risk of expropriation. For all its willingness to work with marginal governments, Orascom follows a strict policy of gradualism, slowly increasing its exposure to risk as it generates trust with the host country.

Succeeding in chaotic environments does not entail making giant leaps into the unknown or just letting things unfold by themselves and waiting to see what happens. Nor does thriving in chaotic contexts require laying down life-or-death bets. Quite the contrary: succeeding calls for innovative thinking and the willingness to go through a trial-and-error process—experimenting to find the right way and increasing commitment when chaos plays in your favor. That is what América Móvil did in Latin America. The company first learned in Mexico how to sell mobile telecommunications services in a market unaccustomed to them. It also familiarized itself with how to operate under a deficient regulation and supervision system, transforming chaotic conditions into an advantage. The easy part was to replicate this model in other, equally fragile Latin American countries.

Or take the case of Bharat Forge. Overcoming the infrastructure and technological deficits in India led the company to important process innovations that challenged the conventional ways of producing forged components, and that, in turn, won Bharat the prime role of supplying premium car manufacturers like BMW or Mercedes. It comes down to this: when facing a chaotic situation, first explore how to benefit from it and then exploit the advantage of being able to thrive where others feel threatened or incapable.

Chaos is working for you when it reinforces your competitive position against potential rivals.

Acquiring Smart

Acquisitions are a great way of growing your company—and of making mistakes. You can choose the wrong target (such as AT&T's purchase of NCR). You can easily get carried away and overpay (like Ford's takeover of Volvo). Or you can make the wrong postacquisition decisions (think Daimler and Chrysler). In fact, it is so easy to make mistakes with acquisitions that a second Murphy's Law might seem to be in play: "If you grow through acquisitions, sooner or later you are going to make a huge mistake that will bring your corporate expansion to an end." Emerging market multinationals, though, argue otherwise, as long as these guidelines are followed:

- Think of acquisitions as stepping-stones for getting to the other side of the river. Watch carefully each step and

181

remember that the real goal is to get to the other shore. Specifically, have in mind the sequence of targets that would help you become a global leader by increasing your size and/or capabilities.

- Smart acquirers act only when they can manage the target better than its current managers (as Cemex did) or when the target can bring valuable resources to the parent firm (as happened with the acquisitions of Tata Communications).

- The cheaper the target, the easier to make profits. Wait until you can secure a good deal. In the meantime, look elsewhere for more interesting opportunities. Overvalued targets can be bought on the cheap if you are patient enough. Move fast when the target is under stress, not before. América Móvil's acquisitions in Latin America are a perfect example of optimal timing. By contrast, Cemex's acquisition of Rinker, perhaps the only flaw in its track record, illustrates how just one mistake can put the whole company in danger.

- Be flexible during the process of integrating targets within your company. Think of each integration as an opportunity to identify new best practices through benchmarking. And remember that cross-country differences in the type of customers, distribution channels, or products can and often do justify differences in management systems.

- When acquiring just for the smarts inside the target— for the resources of the company, technology, brands, or know-how—try to transfer and exploit these resources quickly across the entire organization.

- Don't kill the goose and lose its golden eggs! Every acquired company has smart managers, salespeople, or product designers. Don't assume that you know better than them. Just compare the acquisition of Chrysler by Daimler with the acquisition of Jaguar by Tata.

Successful bidders are proactive and aggressive, but also far-sighted and patient. They know that acquisitions should not be made at any price. Remember what Zhang Ruimin, Haier's CEO, had to say about successful bidders. He advises you to act like a cormorant looking for "stunned fish"—"good companies waylaid, often by circumstances beyond their control."[1] That is why Haier's acquisition track record, both inside and outside China, has been so successful. And don't forget that integration is key. Think how Cemex built an entire organizational structure to handle acquisitions and ensure that two-way learning would take place.

You know you're acquiring smart when you don't feel it is now or never—there's always a plan B.

Expanding with Abandon

The world economy used to be a tranquil pond in which companies could leisurely tread water, knowing that things would change not only slowly but also predictably. Disruptive innovations such as new products or new technologies roiled the water only every few years, sometimes decades. The fundamental features and attributes of products such as photo cameras, automobiles, or beverages didn't change much for nearly a century! (Well, Polaroid tried hard with instant photography, but never captured more than a sliver of the market.)

No more. The new economy of the twenty-first century is a *global* economy, one that is tightly integrated as well as mercurial and ever changing. There are just too many moving parts interacting with one another in complex and uncertain ways. A new innovation arrives just as firms are learning to cope with the previous breakthrough.

Some managers believe that you can't move fast in this type of global economy. They feel compelled to take their time before acting. We've been telling you in this book just the opposite. Speed is the order of the day. You can't afford to stand still; you must expand with abandon. But within reason, and methodically:

- Think that the only profitable response to change is change itself. Never underestimate the need for change, even if things are going well. The seeds of change are to be found in the period of quietude immediately preceding a major disruption or discontinuity. Even a very smart company like IBM waited too long to shift away from hardware and embrace services, although it eventually did. Meanwhile, Kodak managed itself into extinction by not embracing the digital revolution.

- Change is important, but the direction of change matters. You must evaluate where your business is going and what your capabilities are before embarking on a new course of action. AT&T paid $7.5 billion to acquire a presence in personal computers as late as 1991, in a move that few considered appropriate at the time. Did AT&T choose the right direction? Did it have the capabilities to manage NCR better than its previous owners? No and no. Nestlé, by contrast, acquired dozens of water brands worldwide, including Poland Spring and San Pellegrino. It chose the right direction given new customer preferences for natural drinks, and it did possess the knowledge to integrate these brands into existing operations.

- Never expand into new markets where your existing capabilities won't give you the edge. Häagen-Dazs had been successful at entering Canada, Hong Kong, Singapore, and Japan in the 1980s. It then directed its efforts at Europe, where Unilever and Nestlé had access to distribution channels locked up. Instead of fighting not one but two goliaths, it should have focused on other Asian markets or on Latin America.

- Expand with abandon, yes, but not only to conquer and rule. Expansion is also a way to learn, to develop your capabilities, to become a better firm. That was the main difference between Attila the Hun and Genghis Khan. The former conquered for the sake of conquest; the latter encouraged his subjects to learn from the nomadic tribes and peoples he defeated and unified. Expose yourself to new markets, learn through trial and error, develop new capabilities, share them around your organization, and proceed onto the next market.

Great companies grow relentlessly, and without fear of the unknown. BYD could have remained the world's leader in batteries, but seeing the electric vehicle revolution coming, it made a large bet by acquiring an antiquated car company. The capital outlay wasn't the biggest risk it took. The far greater challenge involved exposing the organization to a new industry, a new technology, and a potentially new profitable market. América Móvil also expanded with abandon, anticipating that opportunities in the telecommunications industry come up sporadically and without warning. Ocimum Biosolutions put its ability to integrate knowledge to the test when acquiring companies around the world, but integrating diverse kinds of knowledge was precisely the way to pioneer the offshore lab.

Remember that expanding must be a state of mind, not something you do only when you anticipate success.

Taking on the Sacred Cows

Successful managers are often their own worst enemies. As human beings, we all feel a weakness for what brought us success. We take comfort in what we think works. We are scared by change. We seek refuge in the known and the proven, and revert to being creatures of habit.

The story of the emerging economies and of the emerging market multinationals reminds us how important it is not to take anything for granted, to constantly scan the environment for new clues and opportunities, and to seize the moment of change by changing and adapting. Population shifts, new technologies, geopolitical risks, environmental problems, new career paths, new corporate kids on the block—given the totality of new forces shaping global competition, the future of your company and your own career depends on your not freaking out, really. Stay put. Listen to the chorus of emerging market multinationals and their chanting, and take to heart what they have to say: Execute before strategizing. Cater to the niches. Scale to win. Embrace chaos. Acquire smart. Expand with abandon. No sacred cows!

And one last piece of advice: Have fun. This is a world of vast opportunity. Dive in!

NOTES

INTRODUCTION

1. The data are reported in Mauro F. Guillén and Emilio Ontiveros, *Global Turning Points*. New York: Cambridge University Press, 2012.

CHAPTER 1

1. Jim Collins, *Good to Great*, New York: Harper Collins, 2001, p. 94.
2. *Women's Wear Daily*, April 22, 2010.
3. Building Strong Brands, November 10, 2010, http://strongbrands.wordpress.com/2010/11/10/sara-lee%E2%80%99s-disaster-in-bread/. (Accessed June 16, 2012.)
4. http://www.innovapedia.org/non-classe/bimbos-wind-farm-to-produce-near-to-100-of-mexican-bread-maker/_March 2011. (Accessed September 15, 2011.)
5. Personal interview, Pablo Elizondo Huerta, deputy chief executive officer, Bimbo, September 22, 2011.
6. EIU Global Corporate Achievement Awards 2002.
7. *Advertising Age*, November 9, 2010.
8. Associated Press, November 9, 2010; *Winston-Salem Journal*, June 22, 2010.
9. "Grupo Bimbo," HBS 9-707-521, p. 13.
10. *Latin Trade,* November 1, 2009.
11. *China Daily,* December 1, 2009.
12. MexCham, November 16, 2010.
13. MexCham, November 16, 2010. Personal interview, September 16, 2011.
14. *Flight Daily News*, June 15, 2003.
15. Meeting with Horacio Aragonés Forjaz, executive vice president for corporate affairs, Embraer, January 5, 2011.
16. *Aviation Week*, May 7, 2001.
17. *The Wall Street Journal*, March 29, 2010; *Seattle PI*, December 9, 2009.

18. Meeting with Pedro Ferraz, managing director, Instituto Embraer, March 7, 2012.
19. *The New York Times*, August 30, 2011.
20. *The Economist*, May 15, 2008.
21. *Aviation Week*, May 10, 2010.
22. *Seattle PI*, December 9, 2009.
23. Roland Berger, Soumitra Dutta, Tobias Raffel, and Geoffrey Samuels, *Innovating at the Top. How Global CEOs Drive Innovation for Growth and Profit.* New York: Palgrave Macmillan, 2008, p. 174.
24. *Business Week*, June 16, 2006.
25. Meeting with S. D. Shibulal, CEO and managing director, Infosys, March 3, 2012.
26. Louis Gerstner, *Who Says Elephants Can't Dance?*, New York: Harper Collins, 2002, p. 72.
27. *Seminar*, 485, January 2000. http://www.india-seminar.com/2000/485/485%20interview.htm. (Accessed September 9, 2011.)
28. Meeting with Eike Batista, March 9, 2012.
29. Louis Gerstner, *Who Says Elephants Can't Dance?*, New York: Harper Collins, 2002, p. 230.

CHAPTER 2

1. *Business Week*, July 31, 2006.
2. *Business Week*, July 31, 2006.
3. "Haier Hefei Electronics Co. (A)." HBS 9-308-075, p. 4
4. http://haier.com.cn/news/view.asp?newsid=306. (Accessed March 10, 2012.)
5. Jeannie Jinsheng Yi and Shawn Xian Ye, *The Haier Way: The Making of a Chinese Business Leader and a Global Brand*, Homa & Sekey Books, 2003, p. 90.
6. Yi and Ye, p. 188.
7. Yi and Ye, p. 214.
8. Yi and Ye, p. 216.
9. *McKinsey Quarterly*, August 2003.
10. *Euromonitor International*, "Global Alcoholic Drinks: Beer— Opportunities in Niche Categories," April 2009.
11. http://www.interbrand.com/en/best-global-brands/best-global -brands-2008/best-global-brands-2011.aspx. (Accessed March 3, 2012.)
12. *Modern Brewery Age*, July 10, 1995.

13. *The New York Times*, May 30, 1999.
14. *New York Times*, May 30, 1999.
15. *PR Newswire*, December 4, 2006.
16. *Wall Street Journal*, March 14, 2011.
17. *Wall Street Journal*, March 1, 2011.
18. *Buena Salud*, July 22, 2010, http://www.revistabuenasalud.cl/natura-inaugura-su-mayor-proyecto-de-sustentabilidad/. (Accessed October 29, 2011.)
19. "Natura-Ekos: From the Forest to Cajamar," HBS-Social Enterprise Knowledge Network SKE016, p. 4.
20. *Natura Report 2010*, p. 53, http://scf.natura.net/relatorios/2010/_PDF/ING_PDF_NAVEGAVEL.pdf. (Accessed October 29, 2011.)
21. *Prohumana*, n. 27, September 2006.
22. Bloomberg, April 22, 2005.
23. "Natura: Global Beauty Made in Brazil," HBS 9-807-029, p. 13.
24. Personal interview, October 13, 2011.

CHAPTER 3

1. David M. Potter, *People of Plenty: Economic Abundance and the American Character*. Chicago: University of Chicago Press, 1954, p. 80.
2. Sea-Jing Chang, *Sony vs Samsung: The Inside Story of the Electronics Giants' Battle for Global Supremacy*. New York: John Wiley, 2008, p. 54.
3. Chang, p. 25.
4. *The Economist*, November 1, 2011.
5. Interviews with Yun Jong Yong, CEO and president, Samsung Display Devices, March 19, 1994; and Noh Gun-Sik, president, Electronics Group, Samsung Europe, November 1, 1998.
6. *Korea Times*, October 26, 2009.
7. *Korea Times*, October 26, 2009.
8. Interview, Chang Byung-ju, president, Daewoo Chaebol, June 6, 1997.
9. Interviews with In-Ku Kang executive vice president, GoldStar Co., March 17, 1994, and Min K.S., executive vice president, Hyundai Heavy Industries, March 17, 1994.
10. Interview with Sául Ubaldini, secretary general of the CGT labor union, April 10, 1995.
11. *Academy of Management Executive*, August 2003, pp. 56–59.

12. *Academy of Management Executive*, August 2003, pp. 56–59.
13. *Academy of Management Executive*, August 2003, pp. 56–59.
14. *Business Week*, June 4, 2001.
15. "Arcor: Global Strategy and Local Turbulence." HBS 9-704-427, p. 7.
16. Interview with Luis Alejandro Pagani, president of Arcor, Baker Library Oral Histories, November 18, 2008.
17. *Business Week*, June 4, 2001.
18. Interview with Luis Alejandro Pagani, president of Arcor, Baker Library Oral Histories, November 18, 2008.
19. www.fundinguniverse.com/company-histories. (Accessed March 7, 2012.)
20. *Academy of Management Executive*, August 2003, pp. 56–59.
21. Personal interview, Agustín O'Reilly, institutional relations manager, Arcor, September 9, 2011.
22. Immelt, J. R., Govindarajan, V., and Trimble, C. "How GE is disrupting itself." *Harvard Business Review*, 87(10), 2009, pp. 56–65.
23. *Wall Street Journal*, September 9, 2008, http://www.livemint.com/Articles/PrintArticle.aspx?artid=486D4EB8-7E8B-11DD-9644-000B5DABF613. (Accessed December 3, 2011.)
24. Ibid.
25. *Times of India*, December 29, 2007.
26. *Forbes India*, November 2, 2011, http://www.forbes.com/2011/11/21/forbes-india-reviving-suzlon-tulsi-tanti_2.html. (Accessed December 3, 2011.)
27. *Wall Street Journal*, September 9, 2008.
28. Ibid.
29. http://panchabuta.com/2011/06/17/wind-sector-industry-insightshe-yaozu-china-ceo-suzlon-energy/. (Accessed December 3, 2011.)
30. *The Wall Street Journal*, October 11, 2011, http://www.livemint.com/2007/10/11001206/GE-plans-wind-turbine-facility.html. (Accessed December 3, 2011.)

CHAPTER 4

1. *Academy of Management Executive*, August 2003, pp. 56–59.
2. Personal interview, October 14, 2008.
3. The Chief Officers' Network Infotech, February 6, 2007.
4. *Academy of Management Perspectives*, November 2010, p. 14. Meeting with Stan Shih, October 11, 1995.

5. *Fortune*, October 30, 1995.
6. *Fortune*, October 30, 1995.
7. www.MSNBC.com, August 28, 2007. (Accessed December 9, 2011.)
8. http://www.cmlab.csie.ntu.edu.tw/~chenhsiu/reading/metoo.pdf. (Accessed March 7, 2012.)
9. *Academy of Management Perspectives*, November 2010, p. 13.
10. *Fortune*, August 5, 2010.
11. http://www.charlierose.com/view/interview/9157%20. (Accessed January 5, 2012.)
12. Unless otherwise noted, quotations from Mr. Sawiris are taken from the previously mentioned interview with Charlie Rose.
13. *Lauder Global Business Insight Report 2009*, Lauder Institute, University of Pennsylvania.
14. http://www.charlierose.com/view/interview/9157%20. (Accessed January 5, 2012.)
15. http://wikileaks.org/cable/2009/12/09CAIRO2311.html. (Accessed January 5, 2012.)
16. *India Inc. Going Global.* Collector's edition vol. I, p. 63. http://www.bharatforge.com/press/mediapdf/punetopadd.pdf. (Accessed December 22, 2011.)
17. *Business Standard*, June 7, 2010. http://business.rediff.com/special/2010/jun/08/auto-spec-india-gives-lessons-in-management-strategy.htm. (Accessed January 5, 2012.)
18. http://www.mydigitalfc.com/companies/forging-global-leadership-hard-way-037. (Accessed January 5, 2012.)
19. Ibid.
20. *Business Standard*, April 15, 2003. http://www.business-standard.com/india/news/reshapingshopfloor/129060/. (Accessed January 5, 2012.)
21. *Financial Chronicle*, January 17, 2011. http://www.kalyanigroup.com/images/Financial%20Chronicle%20Coverage%2017th%20Jan%202011.pdf. (Accessed January 5, 2012.)
22. *India Inc. Going Global.* Collector's edition vol. I, p. 66. http://www.bharatforge.com/press/mediapdf/punetopadd.pdf. (Accessed December 22, 2011.)
23. *Bloomberg*, August 28, 2010. http://mobile.bloomberg.com/news/2010-08-23/sawiris-pushes-25-billion-vimpelcom-deal-as-debt-mounts-options-dwindle.pdf. (Accessed January 5, 2012.)
24. *New York Times,* April 4, 1994. Personal interview, October 14, 2008.

25. Interview transcript in Bit, 128, July–Aug. 2001. Available at http://
www.coit.es/publicac/publbit/bit128/perfil.htm. (Accessed March 7,
2012.)

CHAPTER 5

1. *China Daily*, August 2, 2010.
2. http://www.aist.org/news/AISTech_2011_Award_Winners_FINAL
.pdf. (Accessed March 7, 2012.) This section also draws on an
interview with Javier Tizado, CEO, Siderar (part of the Techint
group, March 23, 1995).
3. *NYSE Magazine*, 2005.
4. Personal interview, Jorge Dimopoulos, Tenaris, September 16, 2011.
5. *NYSE Magazine*, 2005.
6. *NYSE Magazine*, 2005.
7. *CIO*, August 15, 2001, http://www.cio.com/article/30445/Business_
Process_Improvement_at_Concete_Co._Cemex. (Accessed
February 4, 2012.)
8. Lindquist, Diane "From Cement to Services," *Strategy*, Vol. 183,
November, 2002, http://www.allbusiness.com/business-planning
-structures/business-structures/330911.html. (Accessed
February 4, 2012.)
9. Ibid.
10. *NYSE Magazine*, October/November 2006, p. 22.
11. *Bloomberg*, November 2, 2009. http://www.bloomberg.com/apps/
news?pid=newsarchive&sid=axVO96o50X10&pos=7. (Accessed
February 4, 2012.)
12. Ibid.
13. *The Economist*, November 26, 2011.
14. http://spoonfeedin.blogspot.com/2008/08/personality-narasimhan
-srinathceo-tata.html. (Accessed July 27, 2011.)
15. http://submarinenetworks.com/systems/trans-pacific/tgn-pacific/
vsnl-acquires-tgn. (Accessed December 11, 2011.)
16. http://submarinenetworks.com/systems/trans-pacific/tgn-pacific/
vsnl-acquires-tgn. (Accessed December 11, 2011.)
17. *The Economic Times*, February 22, 2008.
18. Jacksonville.com, October 19, 2003.
19. *SiliconIndia*, January 14, 2008.

20. *Stanford Business Magazine*, November 2008, http://www.gsb. stanford.edu/news/bmag/sbsm0811/cement_dreams.html. (Accessed February 4, 2012.)

CHAPTER 6

1. *Fortune*, April 13, 2009.
2. *The Wall Street Journal*, January 12, 2009.
3. *Ningbo*, March 5, 2011.
4. *Ningbo*, March 5, 2011.
5. *Fortune*, April 13, 2009.
6. www.forbes.com/profile/carlos-slim-helu. (Accessed June 19, 2012.)
7. *New Yorker*, June 1, 2009, p. 58.
8. Ibid., p. 61.
9. http://en.mercopress.com/2011/02/11/colombian-oil-and-coal -reserves-attract-latam-s-tycoons. (Accessed January 18, 2012.)
10. Amanda Knauer, "Ocimum Biosolutions: Genomics Outsourcing in India." In Mauro F. Guillén, ed., *Women Entrepreneurs: Inspiring Stories from Developing and Emerging Economies*. New York: Routledge, 2013.
11. Knauer.
12. Ibid.
13. Ibid.
14. *VC Circle*, April 10, 2009.
15. *Kromosoft*, July 17, 2008.
16. Ibid.

CHAPTER 7

1. Edward de Bono and Robert Heller's Thinking Managers, July 7, 2006, http://www.thinkingmanagers.com/management/takeovers .php. (Accessed April 19, 2012.)
2. Interviews with Ana Patricia Botín, president, Banesto, November 30, 2004; Gabriel Jaramillo, president, Santander Banespa, February 9, 2006; and Alfredo Sáenz, CEO, Banco Santander, October 4, 2006.

CHAPTER 8

1. *Financial Times*, September 9, 2009.

INDEX

195